Death of a King

Death of a King

An account of the supposed escape and afterlife of
Edward of Caernarvon, formerly Edward II, King of
England, Lord of Ireland, Duke of Aquitaine

by
Roy Martin Haines

Scotforth Books

First published on behalf of the author in 2002 by
Scotforth Books,
Carnegie House,
Chatsworth Road,
Scotforth,
Lancaster LA1 4SL

ISBN 1-904244-00-9

Typeset in Plantin 11 on 13 by
Carnegie Publishing Ltd
Lancaster
www.wooof.net

Printed and bound by
Antony Rowe Ltd,
Chippenham

H. F. H.

Filiae Meae Praecarissimae

Contents

List of Historical and Literary Extracts

Preceding Individual Chapters

[See Sources and Suggestions for further reading for details of editions used.]

Westminster Abbey	John Stow, *Survey of London.*
An Unkingly King	John Trevisa, English version of Higden's *Polychronicon.*
Piers Gaveston Isabelle	Christopher Marlowe, *Edward the Second.*
A note of protest	John Stow, *Survey of London.*
Two variations of an account of royal behaviour in the parliament of 1320	Bishop Thomas de Cobham in his episcopal register.
Extracts from the *Vita Edwardi Secundi*, ed. N. Denholm-Young, London 1957	Anonymous chronicle formerly attributed to a monk of Malmesbury. Conceivably, the editor argues, the work of Master John de Walwayn, senior.

1322 Lancaster after Boroughbridge.
1325 Royal tyranny.
  Guilty men.
  Isabelle's departure for France: a prophecy.

Should the king go to France? Despenser's threat.
The queen's view of her marriage.

A bishop's view of the hazards of matrimony	John Prikehare, clerk of Winchester diocese, appeals to the pope against Bishop Orleton.
Rough justice	Jean Froissart, *Chronicles*.
Edward III's peace is proclaimed	Thomas Rymer, *Foedera*.
Murder most foul	Geoffrey le Baker, *Chronicon*. Thomas Gray, *The Bard, a Pindaric Ode*.
A dramatist's re-creation of the death scene	Christopher Marlowe, *Edward the Second*.
The scene of the crime	V. Sackville West, *Berkeley Castle: an illustrated Survey of the Gloucestershire Home of Captain R. G. Berkeley*.
Rumours of Mortimer's plan to usurp the throne	Geoffrey le Baker, *Chronicon*.

Extracts from the anonymous English *Brut* chronicle:
1327 Pride goes before a fall
1330 And great was the fall thereof

Extracts from a letter sent to Hudson
Gurney Esq. F.R.S. V.P.
by the Revd. Joseph
Hunter F.S.A. (1837)   *Archaeologia* 27 (1838).

In the Text

Illustrations

reproduced in H. Batsford and C. Fry, *The Greater English Church of the Middle Ages*, London 1943–4).

8   Gloucester Cathedral, mid-fifteenth century central tower (author's photograph).

Section 3: pages 116–19

9   Perpendicular work at Gloucester Cathedral, the vault of the retrochoir and the Crécy window, c. 1350 (author's photograph).

10 Tomb with mutilated effigy of Archbishop John Stratford in pontificals, Canterbury Cathedral, c. 1350 (author's photograph), somewhat restored in the time of Archbishop Davidson (1903–1928). Thought to be one of the first alabaster effigies of an ecclesiastic. This elaborate tomb was possibly the work of John Box (John Harvey, *English Medieval Architects*, Gloucester, 1987).

11 Norman work with scalloped capitals in Englishcombe (Inglishcombe) church (from Gurney, *The Gournays of Somerset*).

12 Aisle of St Mark's Hospital Bristol (now the Lord Mayor's Chapel) with effigies of the co-founders, Maurice de Gaunt and his nephew Robert Gurney (Gournay), ancestor of Thomas Gurney (from Gurney, *The Gournays of Somerset*).

Acknowledgements

THERE ARE TOO MANY PEOPLE who have added to this tale for individual mention, but some few such cannot be avoided. Many years ago a student of mine, Eric Wilson, became enmeshed in the intricate web of Edward's doings. Later he was to turn to witchcraft—a theme which finds its place here too. Should this manuscript ever be published he for one will appreciate the length of time it has taken! Most recently Dr A. J. Taylor kindly sent me a transcript of a Public Record Office document, apprising me of the strange coincidence of the pilgrim who travelled from Brabant to the shrine at Cologne at the very time that Manuele de Fieschi was provost of Arnhem. All who have pursued this trail will be much indebted to the late Professor Cuttino's article in *Speculum*, a copy of which he kindly sent me, and which I was to follow up recently with my own contribution to the *Transactions of the Bristol and Gloucestershire Archaeological Society*. The chase has always been interesting, although sometimes it has had to be shelved for long periods. One of the highlights was an enjoyable journey to Montpellier to study the document which gave rise to so much speculation. There is nothing to compare with the thrill provided by an original manuscript from which so much debate has arisen. In short, I would thank all those who over the years, both in Canada and on this side of the Atlantic, have in their various ways contributed to this opusculum.

Author's Note

THIS IS NOT A JEJUNE ATTEMPT at an historical novel but history without the baffling apparatus of footnotes and critical apparatus beloved of the historian but anathema to the general reader, and enlightened by original sources in translation which serve to indicate the flavour of the times. It is my belief that others apart from professional historians and biographers are interested in what history has to tell. The present piece is in the nature of an historical whodunit, set in the context essential for its proper understanding. Perhaps one should give warning in advance that the complete truth of the matter may never be known, though each person can come to his or her conclusion.

Having taught mediaeval history, mainly in Canada, for well over twenty years I have come to appreciate the great advantage enjoyed by those who live in England. Here history is all around us and can be brought to life by the exercise of a little imagination. Most of the places mentioned in this book I have visited more than once and pondered on the scenes they have witnessed. It is to be hoped that readers of this sorry tale will wish to do the same.

R. M. H.
Soundings,
Curry Rivel,
Somerset.

Setting the Scene

Westminster Abbey

KING HENRY III, in the year of Christ 1220, and in the 5th of his reign, began the new work of Our Lady's chapel, whereof he laid the first stone in the foundation; and in the year 1245, the walls and steeple of the old church (built by King Edward [the Confessor]) were taken down, and enlarging the same church, caused them to be made more comely ... The work of this church with the houses of office, was finished to the end of the choir, in the year 1285 ... all of which labour of sixty-six years was in the year 1299 defaced by a fire kindled in the lesser hall of the king's Palace of Westminster; the same with many other houses adjoining, and with the queen's chamber, were all consumed; the flame thereof also (being driven with the wind), fired the monastery, which was also with the palace consumed. Then was the monastery again repaired by the abbots of that church; King Edward I and his successors putting to their helpful hands. Edward II appropriated unto this church the patronage of the churches of Kelvedon and Sawbridgeworth in Essex, in the diocese of London.*

> John Stow, *Survey of London*, first published 1598. From Everyman edition, reprinted London 1965, p. 406. Stow exaggerates the extent of the conflagration.

---

* This was a means frequently employed to provide additional income for religious houses. Resources usually reserved for the parish, the greater tithes, were transferred to the monks for their own purposes.

CHAPTER 1

Ashburnham

An Unkingly King

This Edward was fair of body and great of strength, and unsteadfast of manners and of habits, if men should believe the common tale. For he forsook the company of lords and drew himself to harlots, to singers and to jesters, to carters, to delvers and to ditchers, to rowers, shipmen and boatmen, and to other craftsmen, and gave himself to great drinking. He would lightly tell out privy counsel and smite men that were about him for but little trespass, and did more by other men's counsel than by his own. He was too large of gifts and solemnity [splendour] in making of feasts, ready to speak and variant in deeds, unhappy against his enemies and cruel to his own household (*meyne*), and loved strongly one of his familiars (*queresters*) and did him great reverence and worshipped and made him great and rich. Of this doing fell villainy to the lover, evil speech and backbiting to the love, slander to the people, harm and damage to the realm. He advanced to states of holy church them that were unable and unworthy, that was afterward a stake in his eye and a spear in his side ... But in one point for this king it happened well, that Wales was never to rebel against him. In other sides he mis-shaped himself always. In his beginning he loved Piers Gaveston ... because of him he was reckless of Isabelle the queen and recked nought of the lords of the land, therefore the lords had indignation and put out this Piers over the sea into Ireland.

John Trevisa, vicar of Berkeley, who probably died c. 1402. Modification of his English version of Ralph Higden's *Polychronicon*.

Ashburnham House

*L*ITTLE DEAN'S YARD nestles obscurely in the heart of the English nation's seat of government, Westminster. There church and state, ancient abbey and largely rebuilt parliament building stand side by side. The Yard is approached on the one hand by a discrete late mediaeval archway, on the other by the dark alley of the cloister. Within a stone's throw is the massive pile of the Benedictine abbey. The black-robed monks are long gone, replaced by scurrying schoolboys, but the church is now served by what mediaeval men would have recognised as a college of 'secular canons', priests out in the world, as opposed to monks confined (officially at any rate) to their cloister.

Standing in the cobbled Yard, the monks' inner court, with our backs to the 'Prag clock'—one man's gift to time the impatient feet of posterity—the canons' garden can be glimpsed through the reticulations of an iron gate. On the left-hand side Ashburnham House, outwardly an undistinguished mellow red-brick building, rises from monastic foundations. In its stone-flagged basement traces of mediaeval fenestration and walling are still to be seen, for it was once the prior's house—the abbey's second in command. Passing through the building, which from front to back is surprisingly narrow, one emerges into Ashburnham garden, a minuscule patch of lawn from which on the right the rebuilt 'School' rises like a phoenix from the fire bombs of war. Here, where once the monks slept—for it was their dormitory, many of the great of the land have received a sternly administered classical education. But this place has changed its face for each succeeding generation, perhaps at no time more rapidly than since the Second World War. Straight ahead on the opposite side of the garden stares a blank wall, all that survives of the monastic refectory, which on occasion gave shelter to the mediaeval Commons, migrating for the occasion from the nearby palace of Westminster when parliament was in session.

Overshadowing Ashburnham's tiny garden is the soaring bulk of Henry III's nave, the noble line of its flying buttresses in the French manner somewhat incongruously terminated by the eighteenth-

century Hawksmoor's twin towers. Entering the basement of Ashburnham and bearing to the right the opening door reveals an
unexpected vista of great beauty, the grand staircase thought to
have been designed by Inigo Jones slowly winding its way up-
wards until it passes beneath the *pièce de résistance*, a classical
oval-shaped cupola from the vault of which hangs an impressively
ornate chandelier. The staircase's slow meander eventually gives
on to a dignified suite of rooms, some of them book-lined, the
largest and grandest being the drawing room, its grace only
slightly marred by a heaviness in the mouldings of the ceiling and
by the sad loss, in the early-nineteenth century, of its central dome.
From one corner of the mantelpiece Elizabeth the First looks down
stiffly on the school she refounded, whose Queen's Scholars
still remember her with roses. The anniversary of her accession,
17 November, is marked every three or four years by a solemn
commemoration of benefactors in the same language, Latin, that
the monks had used for centuries and which Elizabeth well understood. Possibly the Virgin Queen has been given more than her
due. Long before her day the almoners of the monastery kept a
school and each mediaeval king accounted himself a benefactor
of that parent institution which lay cheek-by-jowl with his principal palace.

Ashburnham House has not always been an integral part of
Westminster School. In the early eighteenth century the first earl
of Ashburnham leased it to the Crown, to house a far nobler
library than graces it now, that of an inveterate collector of manuscripts, Sir Robert Cotton. There, in 1731, a disastrous fire reduced
many of them to ashes while others were rescued shrunken,
water-stained, charred, and minimally legible, for eventual interment in the recesses of the Department of Manuscripts in the
British Library. To this day they are called forth by those same
pressmarks designed to indicate their whereabouts beneath the
busts of Roman emperors atop the bookpresses in Ashburnham.
It is just possible that had some of those lost manuscripts survived
the story which follows might be other than it is.

It was on a summer's evening that I sat idly meditating in the
comfort of one of the drawing room armchairs. There were none of
Gibbon's bare-footed friars, or even more appropriately be-sandalled

monks, save in the imagination. But, perhaps mesmerised by Elizabeth's steady gaze, my mind became preoccupied with the fate of one of that queen's remote ancestors, a king for good reason not buried in the abbey, that sepulchre of kings, but who nonetheless knew well the terrain just described. An unkingly king, the second Edward; sandwiched uncomfortably between his father, the great lawgiver and hammer of the Scots, and his own son, the third Edward, a mighty man of war and, in the eyes of his admirer the French chronicler Froissart, a paradigm of chivalry.

Between two such national heroes what chance has Edward II of a sympathetic hearing? Does he indeed deserve one? Can he, for instance, be excused as a man born out of his time? Was he an ignoble throwback, a simpleton or a fool, perhaps even a degenerate in the strictly medical sense of that term; a man totally unfitted for the rigours of mediaeval kingship and as such quietly removed to preserve the Plantagenet line? Maybe, to use a modern euphemism, he was a victim of 'homosexual preference' at a time when such preference, though recognised and even excused in kings, was also widely condemned, above all if it was perceived to be the means of manipulation by others in the spheres of politics, government or patronage. These are intriguing questions, but the one which more particularly has baffled historians, both ancient and recent, is the nature and time of Edward II's death. Or could it have been murder? Or, if not murder, was it attempted murder that misfired? Once again history will be seen to be far stranger than fiction. But before this problem can be addressed we need to know a little more about the man and his circumstances. If this sounds just a little like a history lesson, let me not apologise, for this is a very historical place.

CHAPTER 2

Edward of Caernarvon

Piers Gaveston

Edward, now king

My father is deceased, come Gaveston
And share the kingdom with thy dearest friend.
Ah words that make me surfeit with delight:
What greater bliss can hap to Gaveston,
Than live and be the favourite of the king?

Isabelle:

For now my lord the king regards me not,
But dotes upon the love of Gaveston,
He claps his cheeks, and hangs about his neck,
Smiles in his face, and whispers in his ears,
And when I come, he frowns, as who should say,
'Go whither thou wilt seeing I have Gaveston'.

Isabelle:

O miserable and distressèd queen!
Would when I left sweet France and was embarked,
That charming Circe walking on the waves,
Had changed my shape, or at the marriage day
The cup of Hymen had been full of poison,
Or with those arms that twined about my neck,
I had been stifled, and not lived to see,
The king my lord thus to abandon me!
Like frantic Juno will I fill the earth,
With ghastly murmur of my sighs and cries,
For never doted Jove on Ganymede,
So much as he on cursèd Gaveston,

But that will more exasperate his wrath,
I must entreat him, I must speak him faire,
And be a means to call home Gaveston:
And yet he'll ever dote on Gaveston,
And so am I for ever miserable.

> *Edward the Second*, Christopher
> Marlowe, 1594, Act 1, scenes i, ii, iv.
> Modernised spelling

A Note of Protest, Being a Device for Reminding The King of His Duty to His Nobles

In the year 1316, Edward II did solemnize his feast of Penticost at Westminster, in the great hall; where sitting royally at the table, with his peers about him, there entered a woman adorned like a minstrel, sitting on a great horse, trapped as minstrels then used, who rode about the tables, showing pastime, and at length came up to the king's table, and laid before him a letter, and forthwith turning her horse, saluted every one, and departed. The letter being opened, had these contents: 'Our soveraigne lord and king, hath nothing curteously respected his knights, that in his father's time, and also in his owne, have put forth their persons to divers perils, and have utterly lost, or greatly diminished their substance, for honor of the said king, and he hath inriched abundantly such as have not borne the waight as yet of the business, etc.'

> Derived from John Stow, *Survey of
> London*, first published 1598. From
> Everyman edition, reprinted London
> 1965, p. 414.

> This story is to be found under the date 1317 in
> Walsingham's *Historia Anglicana*, from a Royal manuscript
> in the British Library, and in so-called Trokelowe, both
> being St Albans chronicles. In the latter we learn that the
> woman was imprisoned as well as the knight who put
> her up to it. After a while they were released.

Two Variations of an Account of Royal Behaviour in Parliament [1320]

Bishop Cobham to Pope John XXII

Besides which, Holy Father, your devoted son, our lord the king, in the parliament at present summoned to London bore himself splendidly (*magnifice*), with prudence and discretion, contrary to his former habit rising early and presenting a noble and pleasant countenance to prelates and lords. Present almost every day in person, he arranged what business was to be dealt with, discussed and determined. Where amendment proved necessary he ingeniously supplied what was lacking, thus giving joy to his people, ensuring their security, and providing reliable hope of an improvement in behaviour (*morum melioracionis spem firmam*).

Bishop Cobham to Cardinal Vitale Dufour

Besides which, O father and chosen lord, since you are looking for favourable news about the posture and bearing of our lord the king, let me tell you that in the parliament assembled at London, where the archbishop of Canterbury, seventeen of his suffragans, and a great number of earls, barons and lords were present, he bore himself honourably, prudently and with discretion. All those wishing to speak with reasonableness he listened to patiently, assigning prelates and lords for the hearing and implementation of petitions, and in many instances supplying ingeniously of his own discernment what he felt to be lacking. On that account our people rejoice greatly, there is considerable hope of an improvement in his behaviour (*ad spem magnam morum eius melioracionis adducitur*) and a greater possibility of unity and harmony.

> Episcopal register of Bishop Thomas de Cobham at Worcester

Extracts from the Vita Edwardi Secundi

1322 Lancaster after the battle of Boroughbridge

O Earl of Lancaster! Where is thy might, where are thy riches, with which thou hadst hoped to subdue all, with none to resist thee? If thou hadst been steadfast in faith, thou wouldst never have been brought to nought … The Earl of Lancaster once cut off Piers Gaveston's head, and now by the king's command the Earl himself has lost his head.

1325 Royal tyranny

The harshness of the king has today increased so much that no one however great and wise dares to cross his will. Thus parliaments, colloquies, and councils decide nothing these days. For the nobles of the realm, terrified by threats and the penalties inflicted on others, let the king's will have free play. Thus today will conquers reason. For whatever pleases the king, though lacking in reason, has the force of law.

> [An allusion to the legal tag: 'Whatever pleases the prince has the force of law'.]

Guilty men

There are indeed four great personages in England, the Bishop of Exeter [Walter Stapeldon], lately Treasurer, Robert Baldock now Chancellor, the Despensers father and son, who if they are found within the kingdom of France will assuredly not lack bad quarters. For it is asserted that it was by the Bishop of Exeter's advice that the queen's lands were taken into the lord king's hands, and she herself deprived of her French servants. Robert Baldock brought about the ruin of great men. It is not surprising that he is hated by their kinsmen, of whom, though there are many in England, some are in power in France, some thrive in exile, but one and all await the day of vengeance. Whatever may be thought of the others, the Despensers father and son are held guilty beyond the rest.

> Anonymous Latin chronicle, formerly attributed to a monk of Malmesbury. Possibly the work of Master John Walwayn, senior, a secular clerk (Denholm-Young).

Edward of Caernarvon

*E*DWARD'S LIFE is not hard to chronicle, though historians will continue to differ in their opinions as to whether circumstances or his own ineptitude determined that steady, almost predictable decline into ignominy. Much about him was irregular, even his birthplace. Most royal children were born in one or other of a range of palaces that served royalty's peripatetic needs. The Tower of London was frequently a nursery as well as a repository of treasure, of documents, and of prisoners. For Edward it was different. His birthplace was Caernarvon Castle in the remote north-west corner of Wales, a country which his father, Edward I, had at last reduced to submission. It was not the finished castle, the gauntly impressive shell of which still stands. Rather it was a castle in the early stages of construction and excavation, its site overrun by an army of masons, engineers, carpenters, quarrymen, plumbers, indeed workmen of every kind drawn from most if not all of the English shires and from even further afield. The principal architect, as we would call him today, was the great Savoyard master mason, James of St George, a military engineer of genius, whose hand can be traced in the great keep-gatehouse of Denbigh, now semi-ruinous, and perhaps in a dozen Welsh castles besides. Few who have gazed on the massive walls of the great city of Constantinople—as it was called after the first Christian emperor—can doubt the source of the inspiration for the multangular towers of Caernarvon. Indeed, the same type of construction can be glimpsed at St Georges-d'Espéranche, near Lyon, the place from which Caernarvon's master mason took his name. By that time, the late thirteenth century, crusade and pilgrimage had familiarised many westerners with the eastern seat of Empire, which traced itself back in an unbroken line to its foundation in the early fourth century.

But there were other ghosts of empire nearer home. Close by the rising walls of the flamboyantly hostile castle lay the foundations of the Roman fort of Segontium, its glories celebrated with much infusion of legend in that ancient Welsh saga, the Mabinogion. It was a 'British' Constantine who had set forth from these shores to conquer the Roman Empire almost a millennium before. The 'Tower of Eagles', the crowning feature of Caernarvon is believed to have had that imperial bird sculpted on each of its triple turrets, its gilded form reflecting the rising and the setting sun. Here then in this distant outpost of empire the Roman eagle gave place to that of the Plantagenet Edward, the symbol of his new-born imperial power. Moreover Edward I united such imperial memories with the concept of himself as the legitimate successor of King Arthur whose bones and those of Guinevere he had seen re-interred with great solemnity in an appropriately magnificent tomb at Glastonbury. Alas his son, the eaglet, was to prove but a sickly bird unworthy of such pretensions.

It was in the summer of 1283 that work began on the great quay—for each of the mighty royal castles in the ancient principality of Gwynedd could be supplied from the sea—on the castle itself, and on the contiguous walled town which provided, like the bastides of English Gascony, security in an hostile environment. It was on 25 April of the following year, 1284, that the second Edward was born to his father's queen, Eleanor of Castile. The castle could only have been in its earliest stages, so the birth must have taken place in timber-framed buildings erected as a royal lodging. It can hardly have been a peaceful parturition, but at least on this occasion the building works were not overwhelmed by revenge-lusty Welshmen. Four months after Edward of Caernarvon's birth his elder brother, of the unEnglish name of Alfonso, died. And so, by the hand of fate or, as might have been said at the time, by the revolution of Dame Fortune's wheel, the new-born princeling became heir to his father's throne. In 1301 the prince 'that was born in Wales and could speak never a word of English' —up to that time of course—was created Prince of Wales and endowed with all the royal lands in that recent acquisition.

Long before his father's death near the place where the Emperor Hadrian's wall juts out to meet that sand-strewn inlet of the sea, the Solway Firth, the young prince had proved a disappointment. The sins of youth were to be expected, and were therefore pardonable, but Edward revealed traits which were more deeply disturbing. Raised with the prince in the royal household, a practice of twinning immortalised in the *Chanson de Roland*, was a flamboyant Gascon nobleman, Piers Gaveston. His influence proved wholly unfortunate, at least in the eyes of the hard-headed king, so he suffered peremptory banishment, but not for long. When Edward of Caernarvon became king himself in 1307, he promptly recalled the bosom companion of his youth, and shortly conferred on him the earldom of Cornwall with a cornucopia of gifts to support the position. The young monarch's relationship with Piers, whom he dearly loved beyond all reason, shortly became an open scandal, about which bishops muttered darkly and barons more openly, at least among themselves. Some of the greater barons—a coterie of earls who felt themselves forced into factious opposition to the king—by an ignoble trick gained custody of that alien stripling the upstart Gaveston who, sheltering behind the royal dignity, had impudently invented nicknames for them all. Aymer de Valence, the Earl of Pembroke, had been entrusted with the safekeeping of Gaveston, who had surrendered at Scarborough Castle under terms. The unsuspecting Pembroke lodged his captive for the night at the rectory of Deddington while he paid a visit to his wife. The *Black Dog of Arden*, the Beauchamp Earl of Warwick, now gained his revenge. Pouncing upon the defenceless favourite, with the connivance of the earl of Lancaster he had him unceremoniously despatched on Blacklow Hill just outside his domains, where a monument now commemorates the deed. Although the mediaeval rectory which once stood to the north of the church has long since been subsumed by later building—it is now known as Castle House—Gaveston is still remembered at Deddington. A recent grant of arms to the parish council incorporates a crest depicting the unfortunate Earl of Cornwall's heraldic eagle displayed with a chain hanging from its neck.

The king, beside himself with grief and anger, had Piers' corpse, in the manner of a saint, translated to his new foundation of Dominican friars at Langley in Hertfordshire. At Oxford, where the body had rested for a time, a suitably heroic sermon was preached by the Chancellor of the University, Master Thomas Harclay, a Doctor of Theology. Edward nursed a grudge against the perpetrators of this deed until his dying day, by which time the chief participants in the crime had died, mainly by violent means. Although contemporary chroniclers do not vouch for this, a modern scholar has argued that the mainspring of the royal attitude towards Gaveston was not sexual but a natural consequence of their pact of brotherhood (*foedus fraternitatis*), recalling on the one hand the warriors of the *Chanson*, Roland and Oliver, and on the other the biblical David and Jonathan.

Convinced of Edward's incapacity to rule the barons, in this supported by that gaunt upholder of the Church's privileges, Robert Winchelsey, Archbishop of Canterbury, drew up Ordinances for the proper government of the realm, as they conceived it. These they forced the reluctant king to accept under oath and deputed a council to oversee their implementation. From this solemn undertaking a pliant pope was soon to absolve him. However feckless he might appear, Edward had no intention of seeing his regal authority curtailed by nascent notions of constitutionalism. On the contrary, in 1318 he sought to bolster his deteriorating position by seeking papal sanction for his re-anointing with the miraculous oil which the Virgin Mary had allegedly promised to St Thomas Becket in a vision.

If any thought that Gaveston's murder had taught Edward a lesson, they were soon disabused. History may not repeat itself exactly, but similar patterns can be detected. Edward sought a substitute for Piers' affection in that of the younger Hugh Despenser, whose father had been what might be termed a reputable civil servant under Edward I and who had continued to serve the crown thereafter. Hugh was quite different from Piers. After all he was 'English', not 'foreign' or alien, as some felt the Gascon to have been, and that despite the fact that Gascony was an integral part of the king's dominions. Of course, such prejudice was irrational, as by definition prejudices are. One only has to remember that one of the most respected of the barons, fully accepted by his peers, was Aymer de Valence, the 'French' Earl of Pembroke. At any rate, Hugh was scion of an ancient family long denizened in England. His grandfather had fallen by Simon de Montfort's side in 1265 at the battle of Evesham, so from the baronial viewpoint his ancestry was impeccable. True, the family had not yet achieved the highest rank, but Edward was soon to remedy that by creating the elder Hugh Despenser Earl of Winchester.

The younger Despenser's unpopularity stemmed initially from his marriage early in Edward II's reign to Eleanor, sister of Gilbert de Clare, Earl of Gloucester. Gilbert ended his days recklessly in 1314 at the débâcle of Bannockburn, when the Scots, though outnumbered by about two to one, forced Edward in ignominious flight from amidst the carnage of his knights. Altogether there were three sisters, co-heiresses of Earl Gilbert, Eleanor being the eldest, to whom passed the lion's share of the inheritance, together with the most extensive defensive work in the whole of South Wales, Caerphilly Castle. Not this time a castle by the sea, but one surrounded by artificially contrived lakes and moats retained by massive dams. In the present century these lakes have been re-excavated by latter-day lords of the area from the profits of coal, a commodity known but less lucrative in the Middle Ages. More recently, under the aegis of a new proprietor, the State, they were filled with water once more, so that we can regain in some measure the spectacle of the defences of a castle which lacked the benefit of an elevated site. By a strange irony Caerphilly was in 1327 to constitute the last bastion of Edward's power. Another sister of Earl Gilbert, Margaret, Piers Gaveston's widow, was married to Hugh Audley; the third had become the wife of Roger Damory or d'Amory. The two brothers-in-law of the younger Despenser were outraged, not only by the uneven distribution of the spoils, but also by the grasping Hugh's attempt to further increase his power by annexing Gower, for he coveted the title of Earl of Gloucester. They entered into an alliance with the formidable Roger Mortimer of Wigmore Castle in Herefordshire and with the Bohun Earl of Hereford. The Welsh tenants under the leadership of Llywelyn ap Gruffydd, popularly known as Llywelyn Bren, had earlier taken the opportunity to overrun Glamorgan, even capturing the sheriff of the county. Inevitably Llywelyn had been overpowered and equally inevitably put to death, a grievance laid at Despenser's door. On that account the Welsh made common cause with their English enemies in ravaging the Despenser lordship.

From the Welsh border the dissident barons marched to Kingston-on-Thames, from which coronation place of Saxon kings they threatened London a handful of miles away. Overshadowing them all like a threatening storm cloud loomed the lugubrious, indecisive and often petulant Thomas, Earl of Lancaster. This man held greater power in the north than the king himself and once from the battlements of his stronghold at Pontefract had cocked a snook at Edward as he rode by with his army, an unforgivable insult to be mercilessly avenged. But Thomas could not make up his mind, in part because he nursed a private quarrel with Lord Badlesmere, an ambitious baron with an eye on the earldom of Kent. While in London the bishops plied their conciliatory path between the king and his rebellious subjects, opportunity for decisive military action slipped away. One temporary gain was registered. Edward reluctantly conceded the demand that both Despensers be exiled. This expedient was not novel, for Piers had been exiled twice at baronial behest, likewise ineffectually. The younger Despenser turned his talents to piracy in the Channel and captured at least one well-laden Genoese galley. Years later compensation for his misdeeds was required of Edward III, who was anxious to enlist the help of Genoese shipbuilders.

The initiative now passed to Edward. With unwonted energy he seized upon a slight to his queen, Isabelle, refused entry to the Badlesmere-held castle of Leeds in Kent, as a pretext for mobilising a large force which readily secured the capitulation of the fortress by the end of October 1321. Even this did not provoke Lancaster to hostile action. On the king's side momentum was maintained by a brisk excursion to the west, where in less than a couple of winter months Edward was able to subdue the March or Border area. The Roger Mortimers, uncle and nephew, deluded it is claimed by a treacherous safe conduct, were promptly incarcerated in the Tower, while the Earl of Hereford escaped to join forces with Lancaster in Yorkshire. All this was but a preliminary to the final show-down, the engagement at Boroughbridge, where in mid-March the retreating rebels were utterly routed. Decisive in the battle was the intervention of Andrew Harclay, a man in consequence elevated to the pinnacle of his ambition, the earldom of Carlisle, only to be cast down again and executed for his realistic but treasonable negotiations with the Scots. The noble-minded Humphrey de Bohun, Earl of Hereford, suffered an unchivalrous demise, pierced through his nether parts by a Welsh pikeman

concealed beneath a wooden bridge. Lancaster himself was captured, summarily condemned and then executed to the jeers of
bystanders. So cruel a death of one so great—he was cousin to
the king—was to have its repercussions, not only among the
populace who revered him as a saint, but also among others who
read the writing on the wall and were content to bide their time.
The cult of this martyr, both on the Yorkshire hill where he had
died and at St Paul's in London, survived to embarrass his
'murderer'.

Militarily Boroughbridge left Edward and the younger Despenser in an impregnable position. The four remaining years of the
reign have been aptly described as years of tyranny. For those
who survived the holocaust of executions—some families, like the
Giffards of Brimpsfield in Gloucestershire, were wiped out—there
were inquisitions in the hands of specially empanelled justices
who exacted heavy fines. The confiscated lands of the 'contrariants', as the rebels came to be called, helped to swell the coffers
of patronage essential to a mediaeval king. To secure support a
monarch had to be in a position to give. To be able to give it was
first necessary to receive, even by means of confiscation! Edward
and Despenser seem to have pursued the same ends, the consoli-
dation of personal possessions and the accretion of treasure. In
this they found an able agent in Walter Stapeldon, the West
Country Bishop of Exeter, whose rise to subordinate power is
something of a mystery. As treasurer he was engaged in squeezing
more money from those who could afford it, and from others who
could not. But it is doubtful, for all his vaunted administrative
reforms so much admired by some recent historians, whether he
was a creator of policy rather a mere executor. Political motivation
lay elsewhere, with the king—when he chose to interest himself
in business, but primarily with Despenser.

For the remainder of the reign Despenser, the new recipient of
the king's homosexual affections—as many believed—bestrode the
realm like some colossus. It was to him that pope, emperor and
kings addressed their other than purely honorific letters, to him
that agents from Gascony to Wales despatched their communica-
tions and requests, to him that they reported on their return home.
The king was scarcely more than a necessary figurehead, *rex*

inutilis, a man given to rustic pursuits, such as hedging, thatching and ditching, one who consorted with sailors and blacksmiths, loved rural sports but not martial ones, and was rumoured to have been a peasant changeling, for surely he could not be the true son of the mighty Edward, the English Justinian, the great warrior. Indeed, at least one impostor claimed to be the true king on those very grounds. Surely there was no smoke without fire? When Edward appeared in parliament at Westminster it was condescendingly reported of him by Bishop Cobham, and in similar words by the chronicler Trivet or Trevet, that he had behaved himself surprisingly well, cheerfully regarded those present, and shown a respectable interest in business. A promising report, not borne out by subsequent performance!

The apex of the country's administrative system was occupied by a cleric, Robert Baldock, the chancellor or chief officer of state, one of the Despensers' henchmen and close to the King. When the final reckoning eventually came his actions were to receive almost universal condemnation, but none were so shrill as those bishops who had suffered financially at his inconsiderate hands. He was widely held to have betrayed the interests of the Church. Despite Edward's utmost and repeated efforts the pope could not be persuaded to advance Baldock to a bishopric, the accustomed reward for men in his position. Covert stories of his unsuitability were being retailed among the cardinals at the papal court or *curia*, then in Avignon, the gist of which has not come down to us.

At the head of the English Church as Archbishop of Canterbury stood the theologically illiterate Walter Reynolds, reputedly the son of a Windsor baker. Certainly some of his relatives came from that town. He had early caught Edward's attention by his expertise in amateur theatricals, which both allegedly enjoyed, and when the awkwardly intransigent Robert Winchelsey at last died, pope and king connived at the rejection of Thomas of Cobham, the candidate elected by the Canterbury monks, in favour of someone more amenable and malleable. The disappointed archbishop-elect, the 'flower of Kent', for he hailed from a family whose castle at Cooling on the Thames estuary still recalls former grandeur, was a triple *magister* or doctor: of Oxford, Cambridge and Paris. But Edward wanted none of him. He was relegated to Worcester, while the companion of the king's youthful revelries, as well as treasurer of his household, was appointed to occupy the chair of St Augustine. Unlike the martyred Becket he did not change his behaviour on such promotion. The best thing that can be said about this archbishop was that he was devious and compliant, even to the point of trying to assemble the bishops of his province in midwinter to give some credibility to Edward's flouting of parliament by recalling the exiled Despensers. In his own sphere he secured the patronage of benefices by skilful manipulation of papal bulls of dispensation. In the realm at large he did Edward's bidding, albeit not always willingly. Reynolds' duty was to hold regular provincial councils to correct and amend the dioceses and clergy of his province—such was the canon law regulation. Due to Edward's interference not one did he hold.

But if Reynolds was on the king's side, more from choice than from persuasion, other bishops were of a different mind, a fact which Edward was to have cause to regret. Adam of Orleton (a village near Hereford), of whom we shall hear more, was the object of bitter persecution and spent the last years of the reign seeking, as he put it, somewhere to lay his head, while grimly pursued by the pitiless minions of a raging Herod. Henry Burghersh, bishop of the vast diocese of Lincoln, by far the largest in the province of Canterbury, was in only slightly better case. His chief fault was that his relatives had been closely involved in the baronial rising and executed or imprisoned for their pains. Naturally he was no friend of the king's on that account, nor on another more strictly ecclesiastical one, that he strove to keep royal nominees from invading his benefices. It was essential for a bishop to have a corpus of patronage at his disposal, since the clerks in his administration were rewarded by such means rather than by salaries as they would be today. The third bishop in this redoubtable trio was John Stratford, a Warwickshire man as his name suggests, and hence from the diocese adjoining Orleton's of Hereford. In Edward II's view he was anathema for having taken advantage of his position in Avignon as royal envoy to secure for himself the wealthiest bishopric in the kingdom, Winchester, a prize which the king urgently craved for Robert Baldock. Once the virulent attack on the new bishop had subsided his loyalty was ensured by the exaction of 'Recognisances', enforced promises of vast sums as surety for good behaviour. Under this sword of Damocles he endured the rest of the reign, co-operative but praying for better times. These were only the most important of the episcopate who had no love for Edward. It is hardly surprising that two of them, the lawyers Stratford and Orleton, were foremost in devising the quasi-legal parliamentary process whereby the king was to be forced to surrender his crown.

The multangular walls of Caernarvon Castle.

Little Dean's Yard with Ashburnham House on the left.

Painting of Queen Elizabeth in Ashburnham House.

Berkeley Castle

CHAPTER 3

Impending Catastrophe

Further Extracts from the Vita Edwardi Secundi

1325 Isabella's departure for France: a prophecy

The queen departed [9 March] very joyfully, happy with a twofold joy; pleased to visit her native land and her relatives, delighted to leave the company of some whom she did not like. Small wonder if she does not like Hugh, through whom her uncle[*] perished, by whom she was deprived of her servants and all her rents; consequently she will not (so many think) return until Hugh Despenser is wholly removed from the king's side.

Should the King go to France? Despenser's threat

At length this [criticism of Henry of Lancaster's actions which included the erection of a cross at Leicester to commemorate his brother Thomas] was postponed, and the king asked the bishops and nobles who had assembled, what they advised about his crossing to France. But Hugh Despenser the son, unwilling that anyone should advise the king to cross, on account of the imminent danger, is said to have remarked arrogantly to some: 'Now we shall see who will advise the king to cross over to his enemies; he is a manifest traitor whoever he may be.' On hearing these threats the bishops answered the king's enquiry saying: 'Lord, it is known that many magnates of the realm are absent, and it is not fitting for us to give answer in so weighty a matter without our peers.'

---

[*] Thomas, Earl of Lancaster. Isabelle is often described as his 'niece', Joan of Champagne, the wife of Philip *le bel*, being his half sister.

The queen's view of her marriage

[Isabelle] 'I feel that marriage is a joining together of man and wife, maintaining the undivided habit of life, and that someone has come between my husband and myself trying to break this bond; I protest that I will not return until this intruder is removed, but, discarding my marriage garment, shall assume the robes of widowhood and mourning until I am avenged of this Pharisee.' The king of France not wishing to detain her said, 'The queen has come of her own will, and may freely return if she so wishes. But if she prefers to remain in these parts, she is my sister, and I refuse to expel her.'

Anonymous chronicler, formerly termed 'Monk of Malmesbury', because of the provenance of the manuscript and edited as such by Bishop Stubbs. Attributed tentatively to Master John Walwayn, senior, who died in 1326 (Denholm-Young). The chronicle ends in 1325, the year before Isabella's invasion of England.

Impending Catastrophe

*I*T IS HARD TO DETERMINE how far back lay the roots of catastrophe, but it is certain that they were well established by 1325. Such metaphorical roots were of two kinds: persons and places on the one hand, circumstances on the other. In both elements Edward contributed to his own fate. Reviewing the *dramatis personae*, by far the most important is Isabelle, commonly Latinised as Isabella, the king's wife. There has been some confusion about the date of her birth: French sources ascribe it to 1292, a date sustained by most modern works of reference. New evidence confirms the English chronicle opinion that she was born somewhat later, in fact during the winter of 1295–1296. This is significant for our understanding of Isabelle's impact upon political affairs, because at the time of her marriage to Edward II she was barely twelve years old—half the age of her husband. The only daughter of the French monarch Philip IV *le bel*, and of his wife Jeanne (Joan) of Champagne and Navarre, her marriage was in part fulfillment of Pope Boniface VIII's strategy for establishing peace in Western Europe. By this plan Isabelle's aunt, Margaret of France, became Edward I's second wife, while Isabelle was promised to his son. On 25 January 1308 Edward II crossed the Channel for his nuptials at Boulogne in the presence of the French monarch and many nobles. Isabelle arrived in her adopted country escorted by two of her uncles—one being Charles of Valois no friend to England—and on 25 February she was crowned at Westminster. At this juncture comes the first jarring note. According to the Pauline annalist, as the anonymous chronicler from St Paul's is usually described, Edward gave to Piers Gaveston all the costly wedding presents from Isabelle's father. Such behaviour caused her uncles to leave the country in disgust.

Though Edward's sexual preference seems to have been for males, he was also capable of heterosexual relationships. Isabelle bore him four children, two sons and two daughters, the first of whom, the future Edward III, was born as early as November 1312 (Gaveston was killed on 19 June), the last, Joan of the Tower, on 5 July 1321. In addition, Edward has lately been credited with a bastard, Adam, mentioned in 1322. Isabelle's subsequent adultery has prompted an ingenious hypothesis to the effect that Edward may not have been the king's son. There is much that is bizarre about the reign and its aftermath, but perhaps this further arcane complication should be disregarded. Had there been a suspicion of the queen's misconduct it is almost a certainty that one of the chroniclers would have let drop at least an innuendo, regardless of the possible repercussions for casting doubt on the legitimacy of the future king. Be that as it may, little imagination is required to envisage the predicament of a young bride whose relationship with her husband was soured first by his inordinate affection for Gaveston and then, after a short interval, by that for Despenser. Towards the end of his life there is evidence to suggest that Edward had an affair with Despenser's wife, Eleanor.

Indignities were heaped upon Isabelle as in the company of her husband and Gaveston she scurried about to elude the pursuit of Thomas of Lancaster, although the St Albans chronicler reports that the earl secretly sent messages to assure her of his determination to drive out their mutual *bête noire*. The Scots were even less respectful of royal persons. Left near York in 1319 during one of the many northern campaigns, Isabelle came within an ace of capture by a raiding party led by the audacious James Douglas. She was hurried off by water to Nottingham. Undeterred by alarums of this kind she is credited with having interested herself in the repeated efforts to fend off civil war, notably in 1312, when she was but sixteen, and again during the crucial negotiations preceding the so-called Treaty of Leake (1318)—an accommodation between king and disgruntled barons—and in 1321, when the Pauline annalist tells us that she joined the Earl of Pembroke and the bishops on her knees imploring a settlement 'for the people's sake'.

Isabelle's irenic overtures terminated abruptly in the September of 1321. Piqued by Lady Badlesmere's refusal to allow her to enter Leeds Castle in Kent, and by the resulting fracas and loss of life among those accompanying her, she sought her husband's intervention to vindicate her honour. However, there is reason to believe that this incident was deliberately provoked by Edward who with uncharacteristic determination promptly besieged Leeds and in the following month forced its surrender. As for Isabelle, she may well have felt that the castle belonged to her by right, since in 1314 Edward had settled on her the reversion of the property on the death of his stepmother, Queen Margaret, which took place in 1318. Property, in fact, was to be a significant element in the deterioration of the couple's matrimonial relationship. The outbreak of hostilities in the king's continental Duchy of Gascony in 1324 led to the resumption by the crown of Isabelle's English estates, ostensibly in the interest of national defence, since French raids were anticipated. Despite the attempts of some historians to minimise the financial and emotional damage inflicted on Isabelle by this action, it is clear that her irritation was intense. The chronicler of the remote northern priory of Lanercost reported the removal of her servants, who were French and therefore suspect, and the imposition of the younger Hugh's wife on her household. Worse still, the estates were placed in the custody of Bishop Stapeldon, for whom Isabelle developed a hearty dislike.

Such was the unpromising state of affairs when in 1325 it was decided that Isabelle should travel to France as a mediator with respect to the English possessions there, for which her husband owed homage to the new king her brother, Charles IV. Who could have originated such a potentially disastrous plan? A plan made even more dangerous by the subsequent agreement that Isabelle's young son, the heir to the throne, should join her in France. Could it have been the pope and his peace-seeking cardinals, who were urging the kings of France and England to participate in a crusade? Certainly John XXII regarded the queen as an 'angel of peace'. Edward himself was reluctant to undertake his obligations and had pleaded a diplomatic illness. The Despensers, father and son, had no wish to be left to the far from tender mercies of their enemies at home, so they objected to Edward's going. Those who follow the propagandist chronicler Geoffrey le Baker see the whole affair as a carefully contrived web of intrigue spun by the wily Bishop Orleton and his partner in crime Bishop Burghersh of Lincoln, the unscrupulous self-seeking agents of the queen. His explanation is far from convincing. Neither of these discredited prelates could have had the ear of anyone at the appropriate level of government. Yet another straw in the wind is the Lanercost chronicler's mysterious tale (also alluded to by the Pauline annalist and obliquely perhaps by a local Rochester chronicler) that Isabelle was anxious to depart because Despenser with the aid of Robert Baldock and Friar Thomas Dunheved was endeavouring to secure a dissolution of her marriage at the papal court. We may never discover the initiator or initiators of the plan to send Isabelle to France, but we do know that it was eagerly accepted on all hands and specifically approved by Bishop John Stratford—a future archbishop of Canterbury—whose diplomatic experience was once again at the service of the government.

No sooner had the queen departed and with disarming alacrity patched up a truce with her French kinsmen than rumours of her unwillingness to return filtered through to her husband. She claimed to be afraid to do so while Despenser remained at the king's side. With injured astonishment Edward asked how that could be, since at her recent departure she had bidden Hugh an amicable farewell. He himself could recall only one occasion on which he had needed to reprimand her, and that was in private. Isabelle remained unmoved and saw to it that the prince did not respond to the aggrieved letters of his father pointing out his filial obligations. Early in 1326 even more sinister rumours were rife in London to the effect that the queen was having an affair with her husband's mortal enemy, the traitor Roger Mortimer of Wigmore. But first Roger's presence in Paris needs to be explained.

During his reasonably honourable confinement in the Tower with his uncle, another Roger who later died there, the younger Mortimer learned that a commission of judges had passed sentence of death upon him. Shortly before the date assigned for his execution he conceived a bold plan with the help of one of his squires. As a farewell gesture he hosted a banquet for the constable of the Tower and as many of the gaolers as could be persuaded to come. But the food was drugged and as soon as his guests lapsed into unconsciousness the baron scaled the walls, dropped into a waiting boat, crossed the Thames, and with the connivance of John Gisors a former mayor of London, reached the coast, whence he made good his escape to France. The day of his flight was appropriately enough the feast of St Peter ad Vincula (1323). The escape was later to be commemorated in the dedication of a chapel in the Mortimer castle of Ludlow. And so when Isabelle made her appearance Roger was already the focus of a growing band of exiles at the French court. Eyewitness accounts describe how at the celebrations for Charles IV's coronation Mortimer sported the livery of the young Prince Edward, newly created Duke of Aquitaine.

Another visitor to the queen during his sojourn in France was Bishop Stratford. His arrival almost coincided with the precipitate departure of the badly frightened Bishop Stapeldon, sent packing by the irate Isabelle, who considered him to be one of the despised Despenser's minions and hence responsible for her alleged penury. For Stratford she had more respect, indeed some have stated that he stayed abroad as one of the exiles scheming for her eventual return. The contrary is in fact the case. After his mission he recrossed the Channel and returned to the care of his diocese. There is no trace of collusion with the queen. All the same, we would dearly like to know what they had to say to one another in private.

Thus persons and circumstances combined to develop a dangerous threat to Edward and Despenser. Representations were being made at the French court and Charles IV may well have been embarrassed by his sister's impropriety, to put the best interpretation on her behaviour. It was only just over a decade before that the adultery of Philip IV's daughters-in-law had caused an enormous scandal, followed by the barbaric execution of their lovers. In the circumstances we may assume that Charles had scant sympathy for his brother-in-law, still less for Despenser. The matter was taken out of his hands. Isabelle and her party, perhaps despairing of military assistance from France or, more likely, fearing some hostile *coup de main*, took refuge in nearby Hainault where, if we are to give credence to the clerkly Jean le Bel and his notions of chivalric romance, that valiant knight Jean of Hainault, brother of William 'the Good', Count of Hainault, welcomed her as a damsel in distress. The upshot was that the Count, gambling on the prospect of a successful outcome and hence a prestigious alliance with England, to be cemented by the marriage of Prince Edward with his daughter Philippa, provided a body of troops and a small flotilla of ships. Thus equipped the tiny invasion force landed unopposed in Orwell Haven close to Harwich. This initial success was all the more surprising since Edward II was in process of mobilising a fleet from the east coast ports for assembly at that very spot.

CHAPTER 4

Jezebel's Triumph

A Bishop's View of the Hazards of Matrimony

Master Adam [Orleton], then acting as Bishop of Hereford, in the above mentioned public address delivered at Wallingford [December 1326] persistently preached and openly declared, though falsely and with guile, that if the Lady Isabelle, Queen of England, then lawful wife of the above king [Edward II], should go to him in person he would kill her and for that very purpose carried a dagger in his hose [the Latin has *caligae*]. Moreover, if he had nothing else available he would throttle the Queen to death with his teeth (*ipsam ad mortem dentibus strangularet*). By the false and deceitful dissemination of these assertions he aroused such fear in the Queen that she did not dare to approach her husband. In this manner honourable matrimony, which exists for the procreation of children, as also for faith and as a sacrament, has been impeded and many other injuries and dangers have ensued in the realm of England.

> From John Prikehare's prejudiced appeal against Bishop Orleton's translation from the bishopric of Worcester to that of Winchester, 2 April 1334. Winchester Chartulary (MS) folios 4^r-5^r.

Rough Justice

Judicium sine misericordia fiet illis qui non fecerint misericordiam

Let justice without mercy be meted out
to those who have not shown mercy.

He [the younger Despenser] was condemned by the unanimous
verdict of the barons and knights to suffer the following punish-
ment. First he was dragged on a hurdle through all the streets of
Hereford, to the sound of horns and trumpets, until he reached the
main square of the town, where all the people were assembled.
There he was tied to a long ladder, so that everyone could see him.
A big fire had been lit in the square. When he had been tied up, his
member and his testicles were first cut off, because he was a heretic
and a sodomite, even, it is said, with the King, and this was why the
King had driven away the Queen on his suggestion. When his
private parts had been cut off they were thrown into the fire to burn,
and afterwards his heart was torn from his body and thrown into
the fire, because he was a false-hearted traitor, who by his treasonable advice and promptings had led the King to bring shame upon
his kingdom and to behead the greatest lords of England ... besides
that, he had so worked upon the King, that he, who should have
been their consort and sire, had refused to see the Queen and his
eldest son, but rather had expelled them from the realm of England,
at the hazard of their lives. After Sir Hugh Despenser had been cut
up in the way described, his head was struck off and sent to the city
of London. His body was divided into four quarters, which were
sent to the four principal cities of England after London. [In fact to
York, Bristol, Carlisle and Dover.]

> Jean Froissart, *Chronicles*, ed. G.
> Brereton, Penguin edition 1968, p. 44.
> [Here the 'Rome manuscript' of
> Froissart follows closely the account
> given by the contemporary chronicler
> Jean le Bel, who was in England at the
> time.]

Edward III's Peace is Proclaimed. Political Revolution in the Guise of Voluntary Abdication.

In that the lord Edward, lately king of England, of his own free will and by the common counsel and assent of the prelates, earls, barons and other nobles, and of the whole community of the realm has removed himself from the government of the said realm, and has granted and wishes that the government of the said realm should devolve on the lord Edward his first-born son and heir, and that he should govern, reign and be crowned king, wherefore all the great men have made homage, we declare and publish the peace of our said lord Edward.

Thomas Rymer, *Foedera*, 24 January 1327. Translation of the original Old French.

Jezebel's Triumph

*J*EZEBEL, OF COURSE, is an uncomplimentary pun on Isabelle; a contemporary one, since it comes from the pen of Geoffrey le Baker her bitterest critic. But Isabelle's fate was not to be Jezebel's. The thirty-year-old woman had need of the unflinching nerve attributed to her by the chronicler. The invading force which cast anchor on 24 September 1326 was long anticipated and in ordinary circumstances could have expected stiff opposition, even annihilation. No such opposition was forthcoming, but the queen soon gathered recruits, both bishops and barons, including Henry of Lancaster, brother of the much lamented Thomas. Thus augmented, her army moved by way of Bury St Edmunds and Cambridge towards London, but after Dunstable, learning of the king's abandonment of the capital, it diverted to the west by way of Wallingford and Oxford. Arrived at the royal castle of Wallingford the queen issued a proclamation declaring her intentions. At Oxford, on her behalf, Bishop Orleton preached a sermon, or more aptly a political address, which he claimed to be directed against Despenser, but which opponents, anxious to discredit him, alleged was an attempt to drive a wedge between the king and his wife. This was not surprising, since the bishop chose his text from Genesis 3.15: 'I will put enmity between thee and the woman'. Isabelle also despatched agents to London in order to explain her 'cause'. Meanwhile supporters of Edward were also active. In the presence of Archbishop Reynolds, Stephen Gravesend the Bishop of London, and Bishop Stratford, a bull of excommunication which Bishop Orleton had brought back early in 1320 as a weapon against the Scots was solemnly read out at Paul's Cross as though it were directed against the invaders. This proved a transparent subterfuge: the suspicious demanded to know its date. Shortly afterwards, at the beginning of October, the king deserted his largely hostile capital and hastened westwards, which explains why Isabelle modified her own itinerary. She was in hot pursuit of her husband and of Despenser.

The ensuing political vacuum gave the Londoners opportunity to revolt. They seized the Tower, released the prisoners in time-honoured fashion, and in a frenzy murdered the former treasurer, Bishop Stapeldon, who was dragged from sanctuary at St Paul's and killed with a butcher's knife. Archbishop Reynolds who had been endeavouring to consult with his fellow bishops as to a suitable course of action, fled for his life with all the available horses, leaving the more scrupulous Hamo de Hethe, the Rochester diocesan, to follow as best he could on foot. In the country as a whole support for the king evaporated at every level of society—the administrative class deserted en masse. The queen and her burgeoning army hastened towards Gloucester. In that city, according to Baker's chronicle, Stapeldon's head was presented to the triumphant 'Diana'. This seems to be a literary confusion. No doubt Baker had Salomé and her demand for St John the Baptist's head in mind rather than the 'chaste huntress' of classical mythology, for he would not have conceded that adjective to Isabelle. Bristol, hastily garrisoned by the elder Despenser, soon capitulated and the earl was put to death after a token trial.

Edward, the younger Despenser, Friar Bliton the latter's Carmelite confessor, and a handful of others drifted helplessly in the Bristol Channel, offering forlorn prayers to St Anne for a favourable breeze and still recording their minimal expenses in an account book now in the Society of Antiquaries' library in London. Baker plausibly suggests that their destination was Lundy Island, though what they hoped to achieve by landing there it is hard to conceive. To such a pathetic pass had the panoply of kingship been reduced. In the event Edward, recalling his roots, sought sanctuary in Wales, where wisdom would have counselled shelter behind the lakes and curtain walls of Caerphilly. He did provision the castle and it was to hold out until 20 March 1327, when its constable, Sir John Felton, surrendered on terms, one of which was the life of the younger Despenser's son. Edward and Despenser were taken prisoner in mid-November as they travelled in a violent storm between Neath Abbey and Llantrissant Castle.

Retribution was now at hand. Despenser, miserably abused, was brought back in triumphal procession to Hereford, Bishop Orleton's cathedral city, where Isabelle was lodged in his palace. The much later Froissart, dependent on the contemporary Jean le Bel who was with the invaders, purports to record the barbarities of

Despenser's death; his genitals were excised as a sign that he had indulged in sodomy even, according to report, with the king himself. His quarters were distributed to various towns in distant parts of the realm, the customary warning to would-be traitors. Only the royal chancellor, Robert Baldock, remained. Baldock's status as a cleric saved him from such summary treatment. Taken by Bishop Orleton to his London house, allegedly to answer in Convocation for his misdeeds, he was violently abstracted by the Londoners who incarcerated him in their own prison of Newgate, where he died a lingering tormented death. Rumour had it that Orleton connived at the outcome, but there is no hard evidence for that. Edward's fate was for the moment kinder. He was committed to the charge of Henry of Lancaster, his relative, who escorted him to his castle of Kenilworth for confinement with all the respect due to an anointed monarch.

The rapidity of the collapse of Edward's government and of his military force probably took the insurgents by surprise. They now had to face political realities. As victors, their lust for revenge almost satiated, they assembled for the Christmas festivities at Wallingford Castle. Two questions were on the agenda: what was to be done with the king, whose continued existence was an embarrassment, and how could the queen rationalise her continued absence from the bed and board of her lawful husband? We do not know what was decided about Edward and the crown, but from what followed it can be surmised that a plan was concocted to enforce his abdication. To cope with Isabelle's personal position, in the eyes of the Church an indefensible one, Bishop Orleton was deputed to argue that she feared to return to Edward for reasons of personal safety. Supposedly he was given to bouts of ungovernable passion, for which there is some historical justification. The story goes that he had sworn—were no other means available—to 'strangle her [the queen] with his teeth [sic]', and kept a dagger in his hose with which to do her mischief. Whatever the truth behind these politically inspired assertions, Isabelle's intentions were clear for all to see; she would maintain her illicit liaison with Mortimer; the much debated relationship with her husband was a thing of the past.

The political revolution which procured the king's renunciation of his throne and replaced him by his fourteen-year-old son was effected by a carefully stage-managed process designed to give every appearance of constitutional propriety. It was carried through in a parliament summoned in Edward II's name to give it the appearance of legality, its decisions vociferously applauded by the 'people' in the guise of the London populace. The whole affair was master-minded by Bishops Stratford and Orleton, with the turncoat Archbishop Reynolds towed along in their wake. The threat of his son's disinheritance was enough to ensure Edward's tearful compliance with the demands of a deputation from Westminster which purported to be representative of the various 'estates' of the realm. At Kenilworth selected delegates with symbolic gestures formally renounced homage, fealty and allegiance on behalf of each individual estate. It was Bishop Stratford's notary, William Mees, who was responsible for writing down the 'Articles of Deposition', a copy of which has survived. While this was going on Isabelle herself adopted a low profile, retiring to Eltham Palace with her son. This must have evoked some pleasurable memories, for she had resided there in 1313 following a magnificent pageant staged in her honour by the Fishmongers Company. Only one chronicle, an anonymous Canterbury-based one now in a Cambridge college library, even mentions the power behind the scenes, Roger Mortimer, who in the following year was to have his own reward, the unprecedented title of Earl of the March. His ambition and greed would soon surpass even those of Despenser himself. Edward III's coronation took place at Westminster on 1 February 1327, the Eve of the feast of the Purification. For the occasion the volatile factions of the realm temporarily sheathed their swords.

CHAPTER 5

A Dark Deed at Berkeley

Murder Most Foul

Taliter obruitur miles strenuissimus, emisso clamore audientibus infra castrum et extra satis noto quod esset violentem mortem pacientis. Clamor ille expirantis multos de Berkeleye et quosdam de castro, ut ipsi asseruerunt, ad compassionem et oraciones pro sancta anima migrante evigilavit.

That most vigorous knight struck down in this manner let out such a scream that those who heard it, both inside and beyond the castle, clearly recognised it as that of someone suffering a violent death. That scream of the dying man aroused many, as they themselves have testified, to compassion and prayer for that holy soul as it fled the body.

> Geoffrey le Baker, clerk, a contemporary, who wrote his chronicle c. 1350

Weave the warp, and weave the woof,
The winding-sheet of Edward's race,
Give ample room and verge enough
The character of hell to trace.
Mark the year, and mark the night,
When Severn shall re-echo with affright
The shrieks of death, thro' Berkeley's roofs that ring,
Shrieks of an agonising King!
She-Wolf of France, with unrelenting fangs,
That tear'st the bowels of thy mangled Mate,

From thee be born, who o'er thy country hangs
The scourge of Heav'n. What terrors round him wait!

Thomas Gray, The Bard, a Pindaric
Ode. First published 1757 by Horace
Walpole at Strawberry Hill

A. Dramatist's Recreation of the Death Scene

Maltravers	I wonder the king dies not, Being in a vault up to the knees in water, To which the channels of the castle run, From whence a damp continually ariseth, That were enough to poison any man, Much more a king brought up so tenderly.
Gurney	And so do I, Maltravers, yesternight I opened but the door to throw him meat, And I was almost stifled with the savour.
Maltravers	He hath a body able to endure, More than we can inflict, and therefore now, Let us assail his mind another while.
Gurney	Send for him out thence, and I will anger him.
Maltravers	But stay, who's this?

Enter Lightborne [a fictitious character]

Lightborne	My lord protector [Mortimer] greets you.
Gurney	What's here? I know not how to construe it.
Maltravers to Gurney	It was left unpointed for the nonce, *Edwardum occidere nolite timere,* That's his meaning.
Lightborne	Know you this token, I must have the king?
Maltravers	Ay stay a while, thou shalt have answer straight. This villain's sent to make away the king.
Gurney	I thought as much.
Maltravers	And when the murder's done, See how he must be handled for his labour. *Pereat iste*: let him have the king, What else, here is the keys, this is the lake [for 'lock'?], Do as you are commanded by my lord.
Lightborne	I know what I must do, get you away, Yet be not far off, I shall need your help,

	See that in the next room I have a fire, And get me a spit and let it be red hot.
Maltravers	Very well.
Gurney	Need you anything besides?
Lightborne	What else? A table and a featherbed.
Gurney	That's all?
Lightborne	Aye, Aye, so when I call you bring it in.
Maltravers	Fear not you that.
Gurney	Here's a light to go into the dungeon.
Lightborne	So now must I about this gear, n'er was there any So finely handled as this king shall be, Foh, here's a place indeed with all my heart.
Edward	Who's there, what light is that, wherefore comes thou?
Lightborne	To comfort you, and bring you joyful news.
Edward	Small comfort finds poor Edward in thy looks, Villain, I know thou com'st to murder me.
Lightborne	To murder you my most gracious lord, Far is it from my heart to do you harm, The queen sent me, to see how you were used, For she relents at this your misery. And what eyes can refrain from shedding tears, To see a king in this most piteous state?
Edward	Weep'st thou already, list a while to me, And then my heart, were it as Gurney's is, Or as Maltravers', hewn from the Caucasus, Yet will it melt, ere I have done my tale, This dungeon where they keep me, is the sink, Wherein the filth of all the castle falls.
Lightborne	O villains!
Edward	And there in mire and puddle have I stood, This ten days' space, and lest that I should sleep, One plays continually upon a drum. They give me bread and water being a king, So that for want of sleep and sustenance,

My mind's distempered, and my body's numbed,
And whether I have limbs or no, I know not,
O would my blood dropped out from every vein,
As doth this water from my tattered robes:
Tell Isabelle the queen, I looked not thus,
When for her sake I ran at tilt in France,
And there unhorsed the duke of Cleremont.

Lightborne   O speak no more my lord, this breaks my heart,
Lie on this bed and rest yourself a while.

Edward   These looks of thine can harbour nought but death.
I see my tragedy written in thy brows,
Yet stay a while, forbear thy bloody hand,
And let me see the stroke before it comes,
That even then when I shall lose my life,
My mind may be more steadfast on my God.

Lightborne   What means your highness to mistrust me thus?

Edward   What means thou to dissemble with me thus?

Lightborne   These hands were never stained with innocent blood,
Nor shall they now be tainted with a king's.

Edward   Forgive my thought, for having such a thought,
One jewel have I left, receive thou this,
Still fear I, and know not what's the cause,
But every joint shakes as I give it thee:
O if thou harbourest murder in thy heart,
Let this gift change thy mind, and save thy soul,
Know that I am king, oh at that name,
I feel a hell of grief, where is my crown?
Gone, gone, and do I remain alive?

Lightborne   You're overwatched my lord, lie down and rest.

Edward   But that grief keeps me waking, I should sleep,
For not these ten days have these eyes' lids closed,
Now as I speak they fall, and yet with fear
Open again. O wherefore sits thou here?

Lightborne   If thou mistrust me, I'll be gone my lord.

Edward	No, no, for if thou mean'st to murder me, Thou wilt return again, and therefore stay.
Lightborne	He sleeps.
Edward	O let me not die, yet stay, O stay a while.
Lightborne	How now my lord.
Edward	Something still buzzeth in mine ears, And tells me, if I sleep I never wake, This fear is that which makes me tremble thus, And therefore tell me, wherefore art thou come?
Lightborne	To rid thee of thy life. Maltravers come.
Edward	I am too weak and feeble to resist, Assist me sweet God, and receive my soul.
Lightborne	So lay the table down, and stamp on it, But not too hard, lest that you bruise his body.
Maltravers	I fear me that this cry will raise the town, And therefore let us take horse and away.
Lightborne	Tell me sirs, was it not bravely done?
Gurney	Excellent well, take this for thy reward.

Then Gurney stabs Lightborne

Come let us cast the body in the moat,
And bear the king's to Mortimer our Lord. Away.

Edward the Second, by Christopher
Marlowe, 1594, Act 5, scene v. Slightly
modified and with modernised
spelling.

The Scene of the Crime

The visitor having contemplated the Inner Courtyard, will now be led into the Keep through the Norman doorway and will mount the steps into the Keep where he will find himself in the room where Edward II was imprisoned and eventually murdered. This is perhaps the most dramatic story associated with Berkeley in all its long history ... The visitor will observe a deep hole like a well in one corner of the room. This is the Dungeon, and it goes down to the level of the Courtyard outside, 28 feet. It was the barbarous custom to throw the rotting carcases of cattle down into this pit, when the stench of putrefaction would eventually asphyxiate the prisoner in the room above. (This room, now called the King's Gallery, was much smaller in those days, and the air-space consequently less.) Prisoners of lowly birth might be thrown down, still alive, on top of the carcases, but such was not the practice with captives of gentle birth, let alone of Royal birth. The wretched Edward may thus be imagined as sitting in this small room, breathing the pestilential vapours arising from the charnel-well below.

> V. Sackville-West, *Berkeley Castle: an Illustrated Survey of the Gloucestershire Home of Captain R. G. Berkeley.* Derby n. d.

A Dark Deed at Berkeley

*W*HETHER ANY OF THE PARTICIPANTS in Edward's enforced surrender of the crown, or indeed the king himself, seriously considered what might happen next is an open question. Lifelong incarceration for political reasons was no novelty in the Middle Ages. Clearly, however, an anointed king in captivity, particularly in the circumstances engendered by the 'reign' of Isabelle and her paramour, Mortimer, provided a potential focus of disaffection. Political differences in the country were not slow to re-emerge and the coalition which had successfully overturned the Despensers' regime showed ominous signs of disintegration. The obvious leader of an opposing faction was Henry of Lancaster, now restored to the earldom of his 'martyred' brother, Thomas. But it is difficult to pinpoint the moment when Mortimer and Lancaster became seriously at odds with one another.

Developing mistrust may have been a factor in the removal of the king from Lancaster's custody, but there could have been others. For one thing, looking after so prominent a prisoner was a burdensome, expensive and even dangerous task. It may well have been while Edward was still at Kenilworth that the Dominican friar, Thomas Dunheved, the man supposedly involved in an attempt to secure a divorce for Edward a year or two previously, in association with his brother Stephen and a host of others, conspired to rescue the king. The Dunheveds had property on Dunsmore, not far from Kenilworth, so the threat was a local one. Thomas, according to the Pauline annalist (who clearly supplies an erroneous date), was captured at Budbrooke, which is just outside Warwick, hence only a few miles from Kenilworth, and brought before Queen Isabelle. Wales was another potential source of disaffection, and from that direction Kenilworth was quite vulnerable. But whatever the real reason for the change of custody, on 3 April 1327 two barons, Thomas de Berkeley and his brother-in-law John Maltravers, were instructed in the king's name, though he was but fourteen at the time, to assume possession of the captive. It cannot be without significance that Mortimer was Berkeley's father-in-law, although the youthful Margaret was not 'brought unto his bed' until the March of 1328, on which occasion Isabelle and Mortimer were among the nuptial guests at Berkeley.

For their expenses the new gaolers were allotted five pounds a day, a handsome allowance which ought to have more than sufficed to ensure a comfortable existence for their royal charge— less than that sum *per annum* would have maintained a stipendiary priest. Despite chroniclers' tales (informed by hindsight?) of the captive's mistreatment the accounts still at Berkeley show that plentiful supplies of food were ostensibly made available for the 'household of the king's father'. Much of the gaolers' allowance was paid directly from the treasury, but no less than five hundred pounds came from money found in Caerphilly Castle following its surrender at that time. The journey from Kenilworth to Berkeley Castle, the stronghold of Thomas de Berkeley to the north-west of Bristol and close to the Severn estuary, was accomplished with secrecy and haste. So much so, that the surviving accounts of the operation vary. The Pauline annalist shows the prisoner and his guards to have lodged at Llanthony Priory on the outskirts of Gloucester for the night of Palm Sunday, 5 April, and to have reached Berkeley the following day. However, John Smyth, the conscientious historian of the Berkeleys, states that Edward actually arrived at his destination on Palm Sunday about supper time. In either case the rapidity of the journey would have allowed scant opportunity for the melancholy and spiteful diversions which, as we shall see in a moment, Geoffrey le Baker insists upon. The route must have included Stratford, but thereafter a choice of roads was available to the travellers, the easiest from the point of view of gradients being the Severn valley road via Evesham and Tewkesbury, avoiding the scarp of the Cotswolds. The distance to Llanthony would have been roughly fifty-five miles with the short leg to Berkeley from Gloucester about fifteen.

The expense account of Berkeley and Maltravers, later enrolled among the royal chancellor's records for the first year of Edward III's reign, formerly kept at the Public Record Office in London's Chancery Lane but now in its highly automated successor at Kew, leads us to believe that Edward of Caernarvon remained at Berkeley until 21 September 1327, the feast of St Matthew the apostle, on which day he died. This date is authenticated by a wide range of references, official and unofficial. It is, for instance, the date of Edward's commemoration as recorded by the contemporary prior of Canterbury, Henry of Eastry, in his magnificent register, the manuscript Galba E. IV of Sir Robert Cotton's collection formerly in Ashburnham House. It was likewise on that day that the Cistercian monks of Croxden Abbey in Staffordshire—a county which kept the king's memory green by insurrection—promised as early as 6 October 1327 to celebrate the anniversary of the recently deceased monarch. But did the former king in fact die from natural causes as the official sources suggest? After all, he was but forty-three years of age and so far as is known in robust health, despite six months of confinement. Had he required medical attention there can be no doubt that an item indicating as much would have featured in the accounts.

Naturally enough the demise of a monarch, even a deposed one, under suspicious circumstances was not a topic upon which judicious chroniclers would choose to dwell—their own safety might be put at risk. Most are so circumspect as to frustrate inquisitive readers, recording the former king's demise with or without a tantalising hint that by popular rumour it could have been murder (*ut dicitur*, so it is said). There is one notable exception, the Geoffrey le Baker who has already featured in this story. His account, which in Christopher Marlowe's time passed under the name of de la More's chronicle, is highly circumstantial and provides the basis for the dramatist's striking murder scene. Marlowe can be shown to have made considerable use of the chronicle compiled by his fellow-Elizabethan, Ralph Holinshed, himself dependent on Baker. But it should also be remembered that transcripts of that part of Baker's work which covers the life and death of Edward II were being made in the sixteenth century. One of them is preserved among the Petyt manuscripts in the library of the Inner Temple, only a few minutes walk from Chancery Lane. Another is the Cotton manuscript Vitellius E V, while a third, comprising only extracts, was included by that at times unscrupulous acquirer of manuscripts, Archbishop Parker, in his bequest to Marlowe's own college at Cambridge, Corpus Christi, where it is still zealously guarded. It may be added that Marlowe's mention of a wooden door as the means of pinning the luckless

Edward to his deathbed is derived ultimately from Adam Murimuth, a chronicler contemporary with Baker, but infinitely more circumspect and reliable, who supplied the latter with the main thread of his narrative down to the 1340s. So fundamental is Baker's contribution to our understanding (or misunderstanding?) of this affair that the complete passage merits careful scrutiny. I have tried to make the translation which follows as literal as possible.

> These cruel bullies, seeing that death by fetid odour would not overcome so vigorous a man, during the night of the tenth of the kalends of October [22 September], suddenly seized hold of him as he lay on his bed. With the aid of enormous pillows and a weight heavier than that of fifteen substantial men they pressed down upon him until he was suffocated. With a plumber's red-hot iron, inserted through a horn leading to the inmost parts of the bowel, they burned out the respiratory organs beyond the intestines, taking care that no wound should be discernible on the royal body at any place where such might be looked for by some friend of justice and whereby his torturers could be made to answer for such obvious injury and forced to pay the penalty therefor.

It is at this point that the expiring Edward is said to have uttered the cry of agony that aroused those in the castle and the good citizens of Berkeley asleep beyond the walls.

Can any confidence be placed in the veracity of this story, replete as it is with all the vividness only to be expected of an eyewitness's description? Baker, it will be remembered, made no claim to have been present, but he did claim that after the Black Death (1348–1349) he learned what had happened from one William Bishop, of whom more will be said below. A number of doubts leap to mind, even if we abandon from the outset the cynical notion that the form of death constitutes a fabrication of those who felt that it embodied apt retribution—in the manner of Dante's *Inferno*—for Edward's sexual conduct in life. Baker himself was far from that opinion. First of all, heavy compression of the royal body in the manner described would surely have entailed considerable contusion, despite the mollifying effect of the pillows. In any case, suffocation would have sufficed. Indeed this did appear as the official verdict at a much later date when the matter could safely be aired. But arguably this was a euphemism, so gross a desecration of the royal person could not have been made public, at least while his son reigned. Again, it might be maintained that even so ingeniously contrived a mode of despatch would inevitably have left external traces. Perhaps the most telling argument of all is that in an age when lethal poisons were readily available there was no need to resort to such devilish and outlandish methods. Had not Mortimer himself secured access to the appropriate chemistry to facilitate his escape from the Tower? Nonetheless, to this day visitors to Berkeley are shown the now far from fetid chamber— well-lit and remote from the castle *garderobes* as mediaeval privies were called—and in the adjacent passage a 'charnel well', a gruesome reminder of the barbarities to which Edward is supposed to have been subjected. There is also, as might have been anticipated, a ghost to add authenticity to the tradition.

But there are strong arguments to be advanced on the other side. That the tale is not wholly apocryphal is suggested by other more cryptic reports, particularly by the not so reticent version of the *Brut* preserved at Oxford's Corpus Christi College. This chronicle, of which there are a number of versions both in French and English, is so named because it begins with the mythical life of Brutus on English shores. The narrative in the Corpus *Brut* lends credence to the essential features of Baker's embroidered story. It is difficult to discover any direct link between the two chronicles which might explain this. However, before we proceed further along this line of enquiry Baker must be allowed to provide the context for Edward of Caernarvon's last days from which this particular incident has been abstracted. We shall find him to be guilty of a number of inaccuracies and some palpable falsehoods.

To begin at the beginning, that is at Kenilworth in April of Edward's last year, Baker states that Thomas Gurney and John Maltravers were put in charge of the royal prisoner. The official documents indicate otherwise as we have seen. They make Berkeley's responsibility plain, Gurney not being mentioned at that stage. More important is a confusion with subsequent events which causes Baker to mistake Edward's itinerary from Kenilworth. According to him Edward was first escorted to Corfe in Dorset, then back to Bristol, and finally, when his identity had been discovered by some burgesses who planned to smuggle him abroad, he was spirited away under cover of night to Berkeley. During this journey the dethroned monarch was subjected to manifold hardships and humiliations. His tormentors, 'satraps of Satan', put a crown of hay on his head, so recently anointed with holy oil, deprived him of sleep, forced him to ride bareheaded through the chill of the night, and fed him on such execrable food as to make him ill. But of all the stories told, the most fanciful is that to avoid his being recognised his hair was cut off and his beard shaved in icy ditch water which the grief-stricken Edward warmed with prophetic tears: 'Willy, nilly, we shall have hot water for shaving'! Here we have a strange mixture of farce and hagiography. This Christ-like figure meekly endures his 'passion', which ends only when his 'holy soul' is forced to evacuate his tortured body. At that point Edward, whose life had been so ineffectual, achieved glorious martyrdom. We have to remember that when Baker completed his chronicle roughly at the mid-point of the century such 'martyrdom' was widely acknowledged; a martyrdom which vied for attention with the veneration rendered to Archbishop Winchelsey and Thomas of Lancaster, the opposition as it were. Popular political canonisation was a feature of the period.

Perhaps Baker felt that posterity would be tempted to dismiss the more seemingly-improbable aspects of his narrative. In this, at least, he has been proved right. He therefore took the sensible precaution of naming his authority, one William Bishop, whom he declares to have been in charge of Edward's escort during the journey from Kenilworth. This man, he asserts, provided him with information after the great plague, by which time, confessed and contrite, he had done penance in the hope of gaining divine mercy. Did such repentance, one wonders, serve to add religious overtones to his recollection of events long past? However, that may be, there is no difficulty about locating *a* William Bishop, though whether *the* William Bishop must remain in doubt. There was a man in Edward III's service, who in other respects would fit the bill. Admittedly the name is not rare, so we would be rash to jump to the conclusion that he is the right man. In any case, positive identification would not of itself establish the truthfulness of the chronicler's story. Lest the scoffers have it all their own way, let it be said that on another occasion when Baker names his source, this time for the 'abdication scene' at Kenilworth, there is no difficulty about giving his informant an historical identity. Thomas de la More, knight, can be traced as the Thomas Laurence of Northmoor in Oxfordshire who was a relative of Bishop Stratford, 'nephew' (*nepos*) he is called. By a strange inversion of roles that part of Baker's work which treats of Edward II's reign was erroneously attributed to Sir Thomas, Baker being considered, even by that great mediaevalist Bishop Stubbs, to have been merely his translator. Now we no longer search hopefully for that 'lost French original', the mythical 'De la More chronicle', under which title a version of Baker came to be printed—and in the prestigious Rolls Series! The laugh on that occasion was not on Baker but on the modern 'expert'.

Baker's reliance on Master Adam Murimuth, to give him his proper title as a university graduate, has already been mentioned. It is time to be more precise. Murimuth was a canon of St Paul's, hence acquainted with the work of the anonymous 'Pauline annalist'—or 'annalists', for this chronicle is a composite one. Unlike Baker he was a scholarly man with an Oxford doctorate in civil law. Like Sir Thomas he came from a village in Oxfordshire neighbouring Baker's own of Swinbrook. They could have known each other personally. Murimuth's general reliability is demonstrable, though he does employ an eccentric and archaic, not to say an infuriatingly confusing method of dating from Michaelmas (29 September). He is brief, even laconic, and certainly no embellisher of fact or fiction. Were the two chronicles to be placed side by side it would be easy to detect Baker's interpolations and imaginative elaborations. Baker invariably fails to correct the errors in his exemplar. The date of the royal death, 22 September, is Murimuth's mistake—if mistake it is. The Pauline annalist prefers the 20th. In Murimuth's chronicle too we have the lineaments, but only the lineaments, of Baker's death scene. The manner of death is roughly the same, but there is the significant difference of the door rather than the vague 'prodigious weight' substituted by Baker. Murimuth records Edward's stay at Corfe, but in a different context. He also states that Thomas de Berkeley ceased to have direct custody of Edward not very long after his arrival at Berkeley. This should not necessarily be interpreted as sinister, in the manner of Baker, for whom it sounds Edward's death knell, prefacing his confinement in an ordure-polluted cell. The baron can be shown to have been extremely busy with public business and the suppression of widespread unrest, some of it on behalf of the royal prisoner. Berkeley was subsequently to admit his error in delegating responsibility to men, Gurney being one of them, who proved worse than unreliable. It would be easy to multiply the number of examples of Baker's uncritical copying or elaboration of Murimuth, but there is no need to belabour the point. We might sum up by urging that it would be unwise to accept any statement of Baker's about Edward II, alive or dead, without corroboration. At the same time, there remains an uneasy feeling about the fact that sometimes Baker has access to sources of an independent kind which for all we know may point to the truth. Discussion of another aspect of his chronicle, political propaganda, will be dealt with later. For the moment we must concentrate on the aftermath of Edward's death.

An extraordinary volte-face occurs in the government's attitude to information after the fatal date, 21 September. Before that all is mystery and subterfuge, thereafter there prevails an almost embarrassing anxiety to let nothing appear hidden. The impression intended, of course, was that the government of Isabelle and Mortimer had nothing to hide. Initially there was the mode of the king's death to be established. In the Middle Ages, at least among the nobility, the bedding of the bride, birth and death were somewhat public, or at any rate social occasions. By such means a whole range of undesirable ambiguities could be avoided. We have observed the gruesome preoccupation with concealing any mark of violence on the corpse. The reason for that is obvious, what is in doubt is whether such anxiety determined that there should be a murder of the kind suggested by Baker and others. Could it have been a rationalisation after the event to explain why the royal body was unmarked?

Murimuth makes it clear that many abbots, priors, knights and burgesses from Bristol and Gloucester were invited to view the royal body whole (*corpus suum integrum*). Unfortunately he does not supply two important details, the precise timing of the public viewing and the manner in which the (naked?) corpse was displayed. Baker, whose vivid death scene has prepared us for this denouement, unaccountably omits the crucial passage from Murimuth and fails to provide a substitute of his own. The logical termination of his elaborate tale is lost. Lack of corroboration and confusion with the later lying in state at Gloucester have generated scepticism about the substance of Murimuth's statement. This seems unreasonable. Clearly he knew what he was talking about and why it was pertinent to make the observation. Popular opinion at the time and subsequently was that Edward had not died a natural death. The precise date is important because later on the body could not have been viewed 'whole', for while at Berkeley it was eviscerated and the heart removed prior to embalming. What chance then to notice even the most evident signs of foul play? In his customary tantalising fashion Murimuth adds that those who came could not examine the body closely (*tale superficialiter conspexissent*). Precisely how the onlookers' view was obfuscated is left to our imagination. Did Murimuth, we may ask, have legitimate reason for his caveat, and if so what was its nature? Alternatively, is he sowing an unwarranted seed of suspicion in the minds of his readers?

Intelligence of the death of the king's father was despatched post-haste to the government. The Rochester chronicler writes that Thomas Gurney brought the news to Queen Isabelle at the parliament in session at Lincoln. Supposedly that was on 22 September, which would have constituted an impossible feat given the accepted date of death. He adds lugubriously that Edward died 'in the hands of his enemies who had been trying for a long time to kill him'. John Smyth, using the Berkeley archives, records that Gurney was sent by Lord Thomas to Nottingham with letters informing his father-in-law, the queen and her son of what had happened. For expenses he was paid a penny over thirty-one shillings. The young king and his mother appear to have been at Nottingham by 30 September. Of Mortimer's whereabouts around this time we shall learn later on.

While the government was preoccupied in the north with parliament and the insurgent Scots Berkeley Castle continued to house the royal corpse for precisely a month, until 21 October. At this stage our principal source of information changes from the difficult-to-interpret chroniclers to the expense accounts enrolled by the chancellor's clerks. A plethora of facts, figures and names replaces a variety of fanciful reconstructions. It is the world of the administrator and the accountant, on which we have to superimpose our own interpretation. Berkeley and Maltravers continued to receive their fees as custodians, their total bill would exceed a thousand pounds in the money of the time. They were joined on the very day of Edward's death by a royal sergeant-at-arms, William Beaukaire, who was to remain with the body until the funeral. Whether Beaukaire was present at the moment of death is not stated, but the coincidence of his arrival on the actual day is mysterious, since it could only have been arranged some time in advance. The view has been put forward that the close coterie of guards and the fact that the evisceration was not performed in regular fashion by the royal surgeons amounts to almost conclusive proof that a crime had been committed. But surely there were a number of matters to be determined before the corpse could be moved and why add to the expense, already heavy, by bringing another band of specialists from London?

One problem under urgent consideration was the ultimate resting place of the royal corpse. Clearly Edward's interment at Westminster, indeed anywhere in London or its vicinity, was out of the question. There it might have attracted the excessive curiosity and sympathy of the volatile and weathercock citizens, even though they had shown little love for the king during his lifetime. The government had no wish to foster another martyr's shrine such as that at St Paul's for 'St' Thomas of Lancaster. As it happens, we know that a Westminster monk, Robert de Beby, whose expense roll is still kept among the abbey's muniments, was sent urgently to the court at Nottingham charged with the task of securing the royal body for burial among Edward's ancestors. The request was turned down.

One of the most important religious houses within striking distance of Berkeley was the Benedictine abbey of St Peter at Gloucester, now—since the Reformation in fact—a cathedral church. There a *Historia* was compiled, which is more aptly

described as a disjointed collection of material. Its compilation is
attributed to a fifteenth-century abbot, Walter Frocester. In it are
to be found a few not altogether reliable references to the situation
at this juncture. According to Frocester, or whoever the compiler
was, various neighbouring monasteries, such as those of Bristol,
an Augustinian house, also now a cathedral, Kingswood and
Malmesbury would have been competitors for the corpse had it
not been for their fear of Isabelle and Mortimer. Allegedly the
opportunist abbot of St Peter's, John Thoky, braved their wrath
and, as will be shown, such opportunism paid off. Thoky is said
to have despatched a special wagon or 'funeral chariot' nobly
emblazoned with the abbey's arms and to have ferried the corpse
back to his church where it was respectfully received by the whole
community of monks and a procession from throughout the city.
It was then laid to rest on the north side of the choir close to the
high altar, a position of great honour.

The sober facts are seemingly at variance with Frocester. For
one thing, it is almost certain that it was the government which
decided on Gloucester as the appropriate location for the royal
tomb; fear of Isabelle and Mortimer in this context is meant to
enhance Thoky's reputation but is spurious. The good abbot also
omits to tell us that the cost of the carriage's modification, the
repainting in black of its white covering, and the expenses of
conveyance to Gloucester were in fact met by the royal treasury.
It was Lord Berkeley's responsibility to see that the deceased
arrived at Gloucester, after which his concern with the whole
business was at an end.

Between 21 October and 20 December, the day of the funeral,
Edward's embalmed body lay in state in Gloucester Abbey. The
royal council, then at Nottingham, obtained the ecclesiastical
services of the Bishop of Llandaff at 13s. 4d. a day for the whole
period. The choice may have been a deliberately considerate one,
since Eaglescliff was a Dominican friar, an order much favoured
by the deceased when king. Moreover, Gloucester then lay in
Worcester diocese where the newly provided bishop was none
other than Adam Orleton, no friend of Edward. In any case he
was distinctly unpopular with Isabelle and Mortimer and had not
yet returned from the papal court, where he had secured the

bishopric. Also in permanent attendance were two royal chaplains, two knights, two sergeants-at-arms in addition to Beaukaire, and the royal chandler (*candelarius*), who was presumably responsible for the array of lights around the tomb and other items appropriate to the occasion. It may only be a coincidence, of which there are far too many in this story already, that one of the sergeants-at-arms was named Bertrand de la More. There is no known connection between him and the Sir Thomas de la More in attendance at the abdication. Were one to be found we might have another of Baker's informants.

Presumably during the two months' interval before the final exequies the public had every opportunity to see the noble corpse lying in funereal state, although it was doubtless kept at a distance by the crush barriers, of which there is mention in the royal accounts. This was not just a demonstration of the court's confidence in the embalmed body's continued exposure to the gaze of all who chose to come. With the wardrobe, one of the financial departments of state, peripatetic with the court in the north, the exchequer at York on account of Scottish affairs, and the government commissariat—the great wardrobe—in London, there was a considerable problem of logistics. Time had to be allowed for transportation and for the availability of the great of the land.

Despite the misleading statements of some chroniclers no expense was spared to ensure a spectacular occasion. There was an abundance of gold leaf, particularly for the covering of the corpse; the king's painter, John of Eastwick, was responsible for four great lions, heavily gilt and with mantles bearing the royal arms. These were designed to be carried on the four sides of the hearse upon which stood carvings of the four evangelists. There were eight angels bearing gold censers, numerous standards and pennants, robes and tunics for accompanying knights, and much more besides. What seems to have been an innovation in the funerary ceremonial was the carrying of a wooden image or mannequin in the likeness of Edward, to which was attached a copper-gilt crown, a sad reminder of the glory taken from him. All that could be done—some would say to make belated amends—was done, and on the day of the funeral the widow Isabelle, possibly tinged with fleeting remorse, the young king, his uncle Edmund earl of Kent, and a vast concourse of nobles and others assembled to pay their last respects. It would seem that the body of the troubled king could be safely consigned together with his memory to oblivion. Such was not to be the case.

KING EDWARD'S GATE

GAVE ENTRANCE FROM THE MAIN STREET OF MEDIAEVAL GLOUCESTER TO ST. PETER'S ABBEY PRECINCT. THE BODY OF KING EDWARD II WAS HERE RECEIVED BY THE ABBOT FOR BURIAL AFTER THE KING'S MURDER AT BERKELEY CASTLE IN 1327.

Plaque marking the place where Edward's body was delivered to Abbot Thoky.

The head of Edward II sculptured in alabaster.

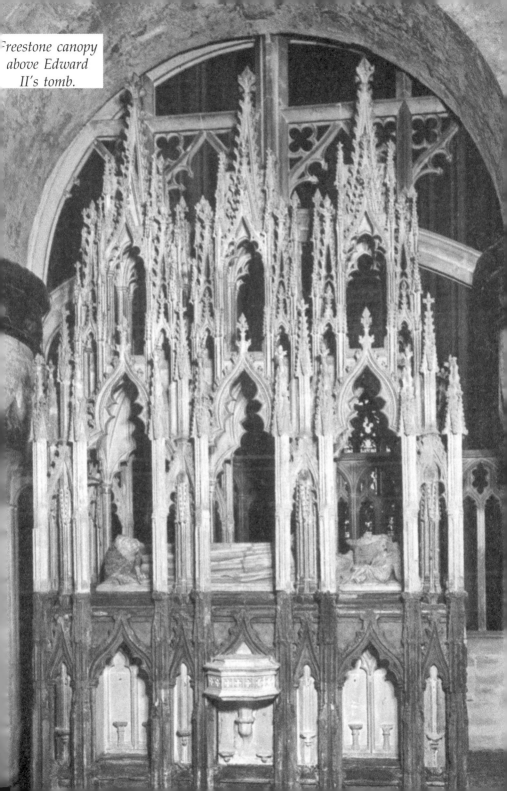

Freestone canopy above Edward II's tomb.

Gloucester Cathedral, the mid-15th century central tower.

CHAPTER 6

Who Killed the King?

To Usurp the Throne: Rumours of Mortimer's Plan

A murmuring among the magnates percolated to the people's ears. It was being said in secret that Mortimer, the queen's lover and master of the king, yearned to extinguish the royal blood and to usurp regal majesty. This terrified the royal ears and the King's friends, William de Montacute, Edward de Bohun, and others, who were conspiring to ensure the royal safety, rightly considered that it and that of the realm could best be procured by Mortimer's death.

> Geoffrey le Baker, clerk, who wrote his chronicle c. 1350. This passage is not in the 'de la More' version which ends with Edward II's murder.

Extracts from the English Brut Chronicle

Pride Goes Before a Fall

1327
The king and all the lords that should govern him were governed and ruled after the king's mother, Dame Isabelle, and by Sir Roger the Mortimer; and as they would all things were done, both amongst high and low.

1328
The king granted that he be called the Earl of March throughout all

his lordship, and he became then so proud that he would leave and forsake the name that his ancestors had ever before.

And the Mortimer then bore himself so high and proud that wonder it was to see; and also disguised himself with wondrous rich clothes out of all manner of reason, both of shaping and wearing; whereof the Englishmen had great wonder how and in what manner he might contrive to find such manner of pride; and they said amongst themselves all commonly that his pride should not long endure.

And Great was the Fall Thereof

1330

And privily a council was taken between Queen Isabelle and the Mortimer, and the Bishop of Lincoln [Henry Burghersh], and Sir Symon de Bereford, and Sir Hugh of Trompeton [Turplington], and other privy of her council, for to undo them all that had accused the Mortimer unto the king of his father's death, Sir Edward, of treason and felony.

The Coup at Nottingham

And in haste there came unto King Edward, Sir William Montagu [Montacute] that was in the castle [of Nottingham] there, and privily told him that he nor none or his company should not take the Mortimer without counsel and help of William of Eland, constable of the said castle ... And that same night Sir William Montagu, and all the lords of the quarrel [i. e. of the plot], and the same constable also, went to horse, and made it seem as they were to wend out of the Mortimer's sight ... And among other things William Eland, constable of the aforesaid castle, privily led Sir William Montagu and his company by the foresaid way under the earth, so that they came into the castle and went up into the tower that the Mortimer was in. But Sir Hugh of Trompiton [Turplington] escried him hideously and said: 'Traitors! It is all for nought that you come into the castle, you shall die yet an evil death, every one of you'. And anon one of them that was in the Montagu's company up with a mace and smote the said Hugh upon the head that his brains burst out and fell on the ground, and so was he dead in evil death. Then took they the Mortimer, as he armed him at the tower's door, when he heard the noise of them for dread. And when Queen Isabelle saw that the Mortimer was taken she made much sorrow in [her] heart and these words unto them said: 'Now, fair Sirs, I you pray that you do no harm unto his body; a worthy knight, our well beloved friend and our dear cousin.' Then they went out thence, and came and brought the Mortimer, and presented him unto King Edward.

English Brut (anonymous) chronicle. Edited F. W. D. Brie, Early English Text Society. Slightly adapted and with modernised spelling.

Who Killed the King?

*H*AD A CORONER BEEN IN A POSITION to review the evidence his verdict might well have been murder by a person or persons unknown. The highly circumstantial testimony of Geoffrey le Baker—as we have seen no witness to the crime nor yet claiming to have been informed of the details by the perpetrators or their abettors—cannot be accepted without support. In view of his overt condemnation of Queen Isabella as a vindictive virago, fear of the consequences can hardly be advanced as an explanation of his reticence to name names. Adam Murimuth simply remarks that the king died, but adds that by common report (*dictum tamen fuit vulgariter*) he was cunningly despatched by the orders of the lords Maltravers and Gurney by means of a heated spit inserted into his intestines. This 'common report' was widespread, being repeated by chroniclers remote from one another, some of whom provide clues as to the means adopted by the criminals. Almost invariably such means reflect those suggested by Murimuth and elaborated by Baker. Only some of this unanimity can be explained away by subsequent copying or the conflation of earlier accounts. We should nonetheless be chary about accepting even so widespread a rumour, the pabulum of myth, more particularly since nobody, however unreliable, seems to have claimed inside knowledge of the horrific circumstances surrounding the death, or even access to some allegedly trustworthy source. All the chroniclers have to offer is hearsay. Incidentally, some commentators have drawn too ready a distinction between contemporary (hence ostensibly more reliable) chroniclers—those apparently writing at the actual time of the events they describe—and those who, themselves contemporary, wrote their chronicles at a later date. Yet we are not in a position to know what notes or drafts the latter penned and pigeon-holed at the time and of which they subsequently made use when writing up their chronicles. Baker's suggestion that he learned of the king's hardships after the great pestilence may for all we know be an artifice on the same level as the words he sometimes puts into the mouths of his 'characters', often as contrived as those of later dramatists.

At this juncture we might be tempted to dismiss the idea of murder altogether, merely concluding that the circumstances of Edward's death cannot be satisfactorily accounted for. On the evidence, and to some extent because of the lack of evidence, suspicious in itself, this would appear to go too far. We shall see. For the present it can be affirmed without fear of contradiction that Edward's departure from this life was seen by those in power—covertly at any rate—as a political blessing. The focus destroyed, factional plotting would fade away, or so it might have been thought.

On the topic of the erstwhile king's lack of medical attention one particular incident is worth reporting. The month before Edward was removed to Berkeley the physician who had treated both him and his wife Isabelle, and who was to be retained in the same capacity by Edward III, one Master Poncius de Controne, an Italian who may have come from Lombardy, was granted no less than a hundred pounds a year from the royal revenues of Northampton in recognition of his services. The peculiarity, if such it be, lies in the timing. For whatever reason, it looks as though the royal patient was removed from the doctor's list in the March of 1327 and the latter given a golden handshake. We would expect Pancius in the normal course to have been called in for consultation in the event of the captive's illness and maybe to have carried out a post mortem examination, presuming death to have occurred naturally. In fact there is no hint of Master Pancius' involvement. He was subsequently to enjoy further grants, which must have left him a wealthy man. Had he been deliberately kept out of the way?

An obvious desideratum for the would-be sleuth is an adequate slate of suspects with convincing motives. In this case he will be disappointed. There is, for example, no list of those comprising Edward's household at Berkeley, not even his confessor is mentioned. Could it be that he was kept isolated and that the food assigned in plenty to the 'household of the king's father' in fact went principally into the mouths of his gaolers? We cannot be sure. Even the gaolers' names are not vouchsafed to us, with the exception of those who bore the chief responsibility, Berkeley and Maltravers, and at a later stage the former's deputies, Gurney and

Ockley. Hence Marlowe's invention of Lightborne. There must have been a considerable crop of underlings. One slightly eccentric translation of Baker provides an astonishing picture of fifteen robust men attempting simultaneously to smother their captive with heavy bolsters, a spectacle which goes well beyond even our imaginative chronicler's intention. Probably two or three persons would have sufficed for the murder, particularly in view of what we are led to believe was a confined space. A castle admittedly did not require a large complement of men in times of nominal peace, but there must have been at least enough to defend the walls, to man the gates, to guard prisoners, and to administer to the bodily needs of those in residence. There would certainly have been at least a rudimentary staff of chaplains to serve the castle chapels (there appear to have been two), where masses are recorded as having been offered for Edward's soul. Are we to assume that he was forced to die unshriven, without hope of that late repentance which Dante suggested would ensure a foothold at the base of the mount of Purgatory? One latecomer to the scene we do know about, the sergeant-at-arms Beaukaire. He is possibly, and if so this is curious, the man of that name, also a sergeant-at-arms, who was among the garrison pardoned with Sir John Felton on the surrender of Caerphilly Castle in March 1327. What was this apparent loyalist doing at Berkeley?

Of course, if Edward was murdered, as we are perhaps coming to assume, the fact could not be stated openly while the political régime soon to be exclusively dominated by Isabelle and Mortimer remained in power. Even if not the instigators of the crime they would still have had good reason for keeping the whole matter quiet. When, following Mortimer's capture and subsequent death in 1330, to which we shall come shortly, something could and had to be said to dispel the three-year-old mystery, the official position was that Edward had been suffocated. In looking for the possible murderers of the king's father, as we should remember to call him, it is essential to distinguish between the agents, those who supervised or carried out the (supposed) fell deed, and the principals, those who were responsible for giving orders that the crime should be committed—that is those with political authority. The latter will be considered first.

Isabelle, Queen of Edward II

In this category of prime movers the foremost suspect is the victim's wife, Isabelle. So far we have seen that she had long feared the violence of her husband, or at any rate chose to maintain that impression for political and personal reasons, as well as to satisfy the qualms of the more squeamish churchmen. Edward's view is plaintively expressed in a lyric poem of fifteen stanzas, written in a form of French known as Anglo-Norman and owing something to the Provençal tradition. The Longleat manuscript ascribes the poem to the king himself, 'Of King Edward, the son of King Edward, the song which he made', though such ascription seems now to be generally rejected. This is how Edward is made to sing of the vanished joys of love and of his fate.

> They've dealt to me a joyless game.
> And 'mid such grief my heart complains
> Of her whom fondly I believed
> A faithful wife—turned to deceit!
> Fair Isabel I dearly loved,
> But now love's spark is dead;
> And with my love my joy is gone,
> As 'tis from many a heart.
> And now 'twere time indeed
> That I in death should sleep,
> Since honours all I've lost
> Beyond recovery.
> And yet why be dismayed?
> What God hath thus ordained
> Full meekly will I bear,
> And serve Him faithfully.

This could well be the rhyming of an accomplished cleric, skilled in literary convention and embellishment. It echoes currents of contemporary feeling which find place in Baker, who likens a sorrowing Edward to another Orpheus softly singing of the charms of his wife, a song made bitter by her 'treachery'. Murimuth charitably suggests that Isabelle sent choice raiment and letters to her husband, while claiming that she was not permitted to visit him. An English version of the Brut chronicle also ascribes to Edward a longing for his family, but repeats the story of his threatening her life, an element that occurs in the poem in which we may perhaps equate the *cerf* or stag with Edward and the *bisse* or doe with Isabelle.

> Go to the Doe beyond *Kenire*[*]
> And tell it her in brief.
> That when the stag is roused to wrath
> And turns upon the hounds,
> She may forgo the leech's care
> Bearing herself so wise.

The person who implies Isabelle's responsibility for Edward's murder is once again Baker, who looks upon the whole train of events precipitated by the queen's departure from England in 1325 as a carefully woven plot devised principally by that 'priest of Baal', that 'alumnus of Jezebel', the 'eloquent traitor' Bishop Orleton, supposed author of a message which sealed Edward's fate. Yet it is difficult to fault Isabelle's alibi. Patently she was nowhere near the scene of the crime and no incriminating instruction of hers has yet come to light, though of course it could have been *viva voce*. Once her husband was dead Isabelle performed all the functions of a widow with punctiliousness, attended the exequies, and was herself eventually buried in her wedding mantle of fifty years before with a belated aura of near-sanctity in the church of the Grey or Franciscan friars in London. There Stow saw her tomb, as he recounts in his Survey of London. Enshrined on her breast, or more accurately beneath that of the effigy (*sub pectore imaginis*), was the heart of her former husband. The heart had been removed, as we have had occasion to notice, while the corpse lay at Berkeley, and there is an item for 37s. 8d. in the accounts for a silver receptacle to house it.

---

[*] The crumbling park? The reading in the British Library MS. Royal A II is *du park q'enpire*. *Kenire* is said not to be acceptable as a form of the name Kenilworth.

Precisely when this heart was delivered to Isabelle is not known. What we do know is that the woman who carried out the evisceration paid the queen a visit at Worcester under the escort of Hugh de Glanvill, the government official entrusted with arranging and paying for the lying in state. The date of this visit is not supplied by the record, but undoubtedly took place round about Christmas 1327, when the queen and her court are known to have celebrated the festival at Worcester. Inevitably there is something mysterious about this episode. Glanvill's original account of 'particulars' merely specifies a seven-day journey from Gloucester to York. Presumably the length of time taken for the journey was queried, whereupon Glanvill was constrained to reveal to the auditors of the Exchequer that at the command of the king (*de precepto regis*) he had made a diversion to Worcester with the eviscerator and stayed there for two days. The consequent alteration in the enrolled account arouses suspicion. Why was an attempt made to suppress this item? To regard it as a 'slip' on Glanvill's part would be to stretch the arm of coincidence too far. It would seem that someone (Isabelle?) thought it appropriate to conceal this particular digression. Why should she have bothered to do so? We can only conjecture, but some observations may be in order.

In the first place the 'command of the king' may be regarded as a conventional phrase. The order may not in practice have originated with the young Edward himself, but at government level as it were. Hence we need not presuppose royal curiosity at this time. Isabelle would not have been anxious to arouse any such feeling in her son's mind, since doubts about the nature of his father's demise could well have redounded to the discredit of 'gentle Mortimer'. At the same time, had the queen been responsible for the murder she would probably not have arranged this rendezvous which might well have served to confirm her complicity. What then was the queen's clandestine purpose? Could it have been mere curiosity? Was she seeking to discover for herself what had actually happened to her husband, possibly in response to some current rumour? If so, at that moment she may either have learned of his murder and even the manner of it or else been told that there was no evidence of foul play. The eviscerator would have known the truth and Isabelle we may imagine was intent on discovering it. It was no formal enquiry, but an investigation for the queen's private satisfaction. It is tantalising to reflect that we are unlikely to learn anything about the exchange between these two women. The eviscerator could have been instrumental in delivering Edward's heart to his wife, though again this is mere conjecture. What actually happened to it over the next thirty years we are left to surmise. Presumably it was consigned to some consecrated place, but not so openly as to attract undesirable attention.

There is one slightly damning piece of evidence. Isabelle can be shown to have provided some benefits for William Ockley, another of our suspects, but in the general tone of rehabilitation, recompense and reward which pervades the early years of Edward III's reign, perhaps this should not be pressed too far. On the whole we would be inclined to dismiss the case against Isabelle and this feeling may be strengthened once we have considered that against her alleged accomplice in crime, Bishop Orleton.

Bishop Adam Orleton

Baker's attitude to Orleton, as to Isabelle, can best be understood by interpreting the misnamed 'de la More's Chronicle' for Edward II's reign as a blatant piece of political propaganda. In the 1330s, and beyond, nobody who had taken hostile action against Edward II, either during his reign or his imprisonment, would have dared to boast of the fact. It had become *de rigeur* to foist the blame for so unfortunate and forgettable an interlude in the glorious history of the Plantagenets on one's political enemies. Baker was without question in Bishop (later Archbishop and Chancellor) Stratford's camp. Stratford was 'uncle' to Thomas Laurence de la More, though the precise genealogical connection eludes us, and as Winchester diocesan made him constable of Taunton Castle as well as assisting his interests in other ways. Nothing against Stratford is to be read in 'de la More' and much more that could have been written is judiciously omitted.

Chronicler Baker may also have enjoyed the more exalted patronage, direct or indirect, of the Bohun family, earls of Hereford and rebels in 1322. This family came into possession of the only complete manuscript copy of his work, including a mini-chronicle devoid of bias against Orleton or that 'termagant of iron' (*ferrea virago*), Isabelle. The manuscript is now in the Bodleian Library. Maybe this connection determined Baker's patent lack of criticism of Mortimer, the Bohuns' neighbour and ally in the Welsh March, leastways until the final stage of the earl's career which is not included in the 'de la More version'. Baker's overall treatment of Orleton is matched by another source, a trumped-up appeal to the papacy launched by a nonentity, John Prikehare, acting as front man, at the time of the bishop's translation to Winchester in 1334. We do not need to enquire into the details of this business, except to remark that it was inspired by the government of the day, that of Edward III, and was a deliberate attempt to fasten responsibility for the more unsavoury happenings of 1326–1327 exclusively upon Orleton.

The bishop proved no lightweight antagonist; he hit back with well directed vigour, and the direction of his thrust is significant. His target was his fellow-ecclesiastic Stratford, now archbishop and chancellor, in close accord with the king himself. Orleton pointed out that it was in fact Stratford who had been responsible for drawing up (doubtless after consultation) the so-called articles of Edward II's deposition—of which he then provides our only copy. It was also Stratford who had given the instructions for Robert Baldock to be brought on that ill-fated journey to London, where he was savaged by the mob. Again it was Stratford who had been prominent among the councillors, deputy-treasurer no less, who had imposed on himself, Orleton, the unpleasant task of justifying the queen's unwillingness, indeed inability, to return to her lawful spouse. To settle the point that the sentiments were the queen's and not of his invention he produced a copy of one of her letters sent from France. It was a brilliant performance, a technical knockout, and accepted as such by Pope John XXII, Prikehare was allowed to sink back into oblivion, despite the calibre of his hidden backers, while Orleton advanced in triumph to Winchester, where the prior greeted him with a magnificent feast and a theatrical performance.

So much for the background. Baker's central accusation against

Orleton is that he sent an ambiguously-worded Latin message to Edward's gaolers. The scene is recreated effectively by Marlowe, who attributes the sending of the letter to Mortimer—in which he may have been nearer the mark than he could have guessed—its writing to an unnamed person.

Mortimer: This letter written by a friend of ours,
               Contains his death, yet bids him save his life.
               Edwardum occidere nolite timere bonum est.
               Fear not to kill the king 'tis good he die.
               But read it thus and that's another sense:
               Edwardum occidere nolite timere bonum est.
               Kill not the king 'tis good to fear the worst.
               Unpointed as it is, thus shall it go,
               That being dead, if it chance to be found,
               Maltravers and the rest may bear the blame.

As for Orleton's alleged responsibility for any such letter, it cannot be sustained. His alibi is cast iron. For one thing, he left London on 30 March 1327, crossed to France within a week, and only returned to England in mid-January 1328 when all was long past. In the interval he was engaged at the papal court in Avignon explaining the political revolution to the pope and cardinals. It would offend credibility to suggest that he could have been in any way involved. If further defence be needed it is ready to hand. At the papal curia Orleton secured a bull for his translation from the diocese of Hereford to that of Worcester. This flew in the face of the government which had other ideas for that see. In consequence Orleton was distinctly *persona non grata* in the court of Isabelle and Mortimer. What Baker has done is to tinker with an almost legendary story. Such a message is said to have been used against Joan or Jeanne, the wife of Philip IV *le bel* of France. Part of Isabelle's family tradition, one might say. Much earlier it finds place in Alberic's Chronicle where the archbishop of Esztergom (Graz) is supposed by such means to have contrived the death of Gertrude, queen of Andrew II, king of Hungary (1203–1235). We can only conclude, I suspect, by completely exonerating the much maligned Orleton and removing another prop from Baker's insinuations against the queen herself.

Roger Mortimer, later Earl of the March

Our next suspect, Roger Mortimer, was to become Earl of the March in 1328, a high-sounding title which irritated his peers. Politically he would seem to have had most to gain from Edward of Caernarvon's death, or at least as much as his lover, Isabelle. Suspicion of his involvement, it has to be admitted from the start, is considerable, but evidence could only emerge after his fall from power. This came in October 1330 when a close companion of Edward III, William de Montacute, launched a commando-style operation. Accompanied by a small group of conspirators he was admitted to Nottingham Castle through a secret passage. Isabelle and Mortimer were surprised in their apartments, the latter being overpowered only after a sharp struggle during which two people were killed. Despite Isabelle's frantic pleas Mortimer was dragged away, taken to London, condemned to death, defence unheard, at the Westminster parliament of November 1330, and subsequently despatched at Tyburn. One of the numerous charges against the earl, almost submerged in the welter of recrimination, was that he had taken upon himself to have the king's father removed from honourable captivity at Kenilworth to Berkeley Castle, where he had caused him to be murdered. For his part Murimuth relates that Mortimer was convicted of consenting to Edward of Caernarvon's suffocation.

This attribution to Mortimer of prime responsibility for Edward's death was to be expected and should not be admitted without due consideration of the circumstances. The accused was given no opportunity to rebut the charge, yet there was an established practice of imputing all manner of hideous crimes to those summarily convicted in this way. The 'trials' of the younger Despenser and of Thomas of Lancaster provide illustration enough. In this case, however, there is supporting documentation of exceptional interest, which ostensibly throws unexpected light on Mortimer's participation. It comes in the form of a record of judicial proceedings before the justices of the court of King's Bench.

Mortimer had been justice of North Wales and on his death was succeeded in that position by Sir John Wysham, himself a Mortimer partisan who in 1328–1329 had occupied the important position of steward of the royal household. The new justice may well have been embarrassed by a forthright 'appeal' or accusation brought before him in 1330 and levelled against William Shalford, Mortimer's deputy justice at the time of Edward of Caernarvon's death. The appellant was Howel ap Gruffydd, who was almost too well supported by an extensive array of fellow Welshmen. The charge was no less than that of compassing the death of the former king. Shalford was alleged to have sent a letter from Rhosfair in Anglesey warning his principal, Mortimer, then at Abergavenny in the south of the country, of the hatching of conspiracies in both North and South Wales in collusion with important persons in England. Their purpose, as may be guessed, was to spring Edward from his prison at Berkeley. Shalford is stated to have warned his correspondent that were the conspirators to be successful Mortimer and his supporters would be destroyed—a somewhat superfluous corollary one would have thought. He therefore counselled him to act in such a way as to ensure that no one either in Wales or England would have further occasion to consider Edward's deliverance (*ne nul autre Dengleterre ne de Gales averoient matere de penser de sa deliveraunce*). Mortimer at once showed the letter to William Ockley, of whom we shall hear more, with instructions to carry it to Berkeley. There he was to allow Edward's custodians to examine it and to charge them to respond appropriately to the contents. Without fail they were to provide immediate remedy. Ockley, so the accusation continues, undertook the mission and together with those who were supposed to be guarding the lord Edward traitorously slew him.

This was an explosive matter, so the case was referred to the court of King's Bench. Following the initial summons the appellant, who claimed that he was delayed at Worcester by illness, failed to put in an appearance. Subsequently both parties were dismissed *sine die*, that is without a further hearing. Howel had hoped to have the matter resolved on his home ground, with his backers on hand, and objected to the jurisdiction of the English court. The difficulty was that the appeal involved not only Wales but also England, Berkeley that is. The whole affair was allowed to fizzle out. The proceedings were however examined in Chancery, where in October 1331 the appeal was described as one that could not be brought to a final issue in King's Bench. Judgment was therefore given for the defendant.

What is to be made of this? On the face of it Shalford was the instigator of the crime, Mortimer the man responsible for relaying the suggestion of murder, without himself having to risk a separate written instruction, while Ockley combined with those at Berkeley to perpetrate the deed. The solution is final, but far too neat in its tying up of loose ends. Were the Welsh trying to get their own back on Mortimer's remaining henchmen? Mortimer himself was dead, Ockley had fled. Where was corroboration or denial to come from? The mysterious letter with its covert implications is surely just another variation on a familiar theme. Like Baker's work the accusation is strikingly circumstantial, yet who in Wales would have known of these 'facts', let alone have transcribed the letter? In addition, it is interesting to note that one of the sureties for the defendant, Shalford, was a John de Eccleshale of Staffordshire, a particularly close friend of Stratford and mentioned in his will. What was he doing 'on the wrong side', as it were? The answer, one suspects, is fairly clear. His attitude was a reflection of the government's view that nothing was to be gained by stirring up mud and that the whole matter was more than suspect. In fact it is likely to have been a 'put up job'. An entry of 10 May 1331 on the patent rolls shows that Shalford was appointed a commissioner to examine the complaints of Englishmen in North Wales who claimed to be oppressed by Sir Rhys ap Gruffydd. This is the very man named in the appeal as one of the supporters of the former king, whose loyalty never wavered. Edward III undoubtedly did not consider Shalford blameworthy, for in 1331 he was acting as the royal keeper of Mortimer's lands throughout Wales, the March, and neighbouring counties and in the following year he was deputed to collect ships in North Wales for the king's projected passage to Ireland. It appears that we can strike Shalford from our list of suspects and relegate Howel's story to the realm of myth. That does not mean to say, however, that it has no kernel of truth.

One would not say that the evidence against Mortimer has

totally collapsed, but rather that its reliability has been seriously impugned. It is necessary to remember that to all intents and purposes he constituted the ultimate political authority in the land and that he could have ordered Edward's death by word of mouth, a means which would have left no trace—a man technically innocent because he could not be proved guilty. We must now come to those closer to the prisoner—and first the gaoler-in-chief, Thomas de Berkeley.

Thomas de Berkeley, Lord of Berkeley

We have already heard a lot about Berkeley. His position would dictate that he could not avoid overall accountability for Edward of Caernarvon's fate. The Westminster parliament which condemned Mortimer turned next to an assessment of Berkeley's culpability. The defendant's initial affirmation is at first glance quite astonishing. He alleged that before the meeting of that particular parliament he knew nothing about the former king's death. The Latin is enigmatic: *Nec unquam de morte sua usque in presenti parliamento isto.* Now this can hardly be taken to mean, as some have thought, that the baron did not know that the king was dead. For one thing such a statement would have been tantamount to treason, and had been so interpreted during the regime of Isabelle and Mortimer; for another, it would be quite inconceivable in the light of all the circumstances already painstakingly reviewed. What Berkeley meant to say, and he ought to have expressed himself more clearly, unless the recording clerk is to blame, was that he knew nothing about the circumstances of Edward's death. As we now know, the idea of murder was first openly mooted in the parliament and there accepted as the cause of death.

Unfortunately for his reputation as a truthful man the baron went on to state that he had not been at Berkeley on 21 September but some few miles away at his property of Bradley by Wotton-under-Edge. There he was allegedly so ill that for a while he lost his memory! Such opportune sickness, and convenient amnesia, were not accepted as an excuse for his negligence; he would have to answer for the death of the captive entrusted to him. Berkeley replied that he had associated with Maltravers keepers and servants in whom he placed as much trust as in himself. For proof of his assertion he 'put himself on the country', that is to say to the decision of a jury. Twelve knights were empanelled who declared on oath that Berkeley was not guilty of the murder and that he neither assented to it nor provided assistance. They confirmed that his life was despaired of at Bradley and denied that he had fled or absented himself to facilitate the murder. This was an excellent verdict for Berkeley and we need not go into the possible reasons for it or to discuss why the baron did not insist on the right to be judged by his peers—men of the same rank as himself. Nonetheless, it was not considered adequate for dismissal of the case. Because he had appointed Thomas Gurney and William Ockley as deputy keepers, by whom the former king was murdered, he would have to respond in the next parliament. Meanwhile he was to remain in the custody of Ralph Neville, steward of the household. At the petition of his peers he was subsequently bailed. The matter dragged on until the York parliament of 1335. There the proceedings were revived, but the lords were even then reluctant to determine the issue, preferring to leave the matter to the king's pleasure. Edward, seeing that Berkeley had been found not guilty on the principal charge, allowed him to depart *sine die*, but he reserved the right to revive the matter at a later parliament. At long last on 16 March 1337, at the Westminster parliament, Berkeley was finally acquitted with only a slight stain on his character—he had to some degree been negligent.

But was Berkeley in fact innocent of the crime? The family's historian, John Smyth, completely destroyed Thomas's alibi with evidence from the baron's own household accounts. These showed that he did not in fact reach Bradley until a week after Edward of Caernarvon's death, 28 September. As to his memory, it was not so defective as to prevent him from writing letters and sending them by Gurney, as we have already seen, to the court at Nottingham. His 'recovery' was sufficiently rapid as to enable him to attend the royal corpse on its journey to Gloucester and even to indulge in some hunting and hawking. If his illness seems to have been contrived, more damning still is the evidence which

Smyth produces to the effect that when the blow fell he concealed Gurney and provided him with money for his flight. Smyth becomes quite incensed by the 'notorious lie' of the Tudor historian, Polydore Vergil, to the effect that Berkeley was 'executed for the treason of murdering the king', yet he himself produces evidence that would have ensured that very outcome. There are a number of loose ends here, but the case against Berkeley remains compelling. Could there have been some secret understanding with his father-in-law? We have no evidence.

John Maltravers, of Lytchett in Dorset

John Maltravers is the last of the greater men in the case. The manner of his treatment is quite extraordinary even by the measure of the story we have been unravelling. He was never formally accused of Edward of Caernarvon's death, despite the fact that he remained at Berkeley throughout the crucial period and could hardly have been ignorant of what was afoot. In the parliament of 1330 he was arraigned and condemned to death on quite another count, consideration of which must be postponed for a moment. Serious as it was, we can hardly believe that this other offence should have taken precedence over Edward's murder. In any case, an accumulation of charges was regular practice, as we have noticed in some other cases.

Sir Thomas Gurney of Somerset and William Ockley or Ogle

Two suspects remain, Sir Thomas Gurney and William Ockley, sometimes called Ogle. Of both we have heard something already. They can conveniently be treated together, since they were jointly condemned to death at the Westminster parliament of 1330 for 'traitorously murdering the king's father'. Their part in the affair, so far as documentary evidence goes, is obscure. According to his defence in parliament Berkeley deputed them both, but unhelpfully he omits to say when. Public affairs, the perennial task of maintaining law and order frequently called the baron from his home, so it need not necessarily have been immediately prior to

Edward of Caernarvon's death. Indeed, Baker associates Gurney (whom he calls Corneye) with the pillorying of Edward on the way to Berkeley. But if we are to credit Howel ap Gruffydd's accusation Ockley could only have arrived at Berkeley (for the first time?) shortly before the day of the murder. According to Howel, Shalford's letter was dated 14 September 1327 from Anglesey. How could he have known? With hard riding and given favourable weather the bearer must have taken at least four days to reach Abergavenny over difficult Welsh terrain. Supposing Ockley had set out the day after the messenger's arrival, he could just about have reached Berkeley on the 20th. This would seem to imply that his appointment as gaoler by Thomas de Berkeley was a last-minute affair. Of course, it is possible that Ockley had been at Berkeley previously and was only paying a visit to Mortimer at Abergavenny, but that is to rely on hypothesis. The Shalford letter gives no hint of anything of the sort. So far as the evidence goes—that means reliance on Howel ap Gruffydd— Ockley was, like Beaukaire, a latecomer to Berkeley. It follows that Lord Berkeley was covering up the fact when he admitted to making Ockley one of his deputies.

There is a further point. Have we any confirmation of Mortimer's presence at Abergavenny? The court and the core of the bureaucracy of chancery and other clerks were at Lincoln, to which place parliament was summoned for the morrow of the Exaltation of the Holy Cross, that is 15 September 1327. Perhaps only the queen and her son had arrived there, but if so this would pose a slight difficulty since Smyth supposes that Gurney's journey to Nottingham immediately after the murder was to deliver letters to Berkeley's father-in-law in addition to Isabelle and the young Edward. Smyth also states, and there must be something wrong with this, that 'by a second direction brought back by Gurney [Berkeley] kept secret the king's death till All Saints [1 November] following'. It has been demonstrated that there was no conceal-ment of the royal death, quite the reverse. Had Mortimer been at both Abergavenny and Nottingham at the appropriate times in September he must have left the former immediately after bidding farewell to the rapidly departing Ockley.

Mutual contacts

Finally, just a little needs to be said about the background and previous mutual contact of some of our suspects. We have had occasion to note often enough that Thomas de Berkeley and John Maltravers were brothers-in-law, who clearly had known each other well for some considerable time. Both had suffered at the hands of Edward II with some justification. Berkeley and his brother Maurice, as well as their father, also called Maurice, had all been imprisoned during Edward's reign and the Berkeley lands had been confiscated. Maltravers was a Dorset baron who, to judge from the mandates directed to various sheriffs at the time of the restoration of his estates in 1327, also possessed property in Oxfordshire, Berkshire, Somersetshire and Wiltshire. In 1319 he had been associated with the Berkeleys and with Thomas Gurney, a knight who was a neighbour of his in Somersetshire, in the breaching of the park at Painswick belonging to the earl of Pembroke, Aymer de Valence, causing a massive amount of damage there—including the killing of numerous deer. Whether this had any political significance, was the consequence of some local quarrel, or just an act of sheer lawlessness, is not at present clear. Previously the Berkeleys had been among Pembroke's retainers. But it has been suggested that Maurice de Berkeley senior (father of Thomas) could have been irritated by his failure to secure any of the Clare inheritance by right of his wife Isabel, a daughter by a first marriage of the Gilbert de Clare who had died at Bannockburn in 1314. Pembroke was influential at court but apparently had not supported his retainer in this matter.

Maltravers was with Mortimer and the earl of Hereford for the burning of the town of Bridgnorth during the 1321–1322 rebellion, which followed only a short time after he had received a pardon for acting against the Despensers. Pardoned again in 1324 with restoration of his lands, he was forced to enter into recognisances both with the king and the elder Despenser. In short, all these men had a history of violent behaviour, in itself not unusual at the time, as well as of rebellion against Edward. On that account they had suffered confiscation or imprisonment, sometimes both.

That they had little affection for the king, let alone loyalty, would be a reasonable deduction.

The odd man out is William Ockley, who is difficult to track down. There does not seem to have been any early connection between him and the others, which is scarcely surprising since his estates appear to have been in Ireland. In 1329 he was keeper of the manor of Ellesmere in Shropshire, part of the considerable property which had newly passed to Queen Isabelle 'by royal grant'. This is obviously a mark of the favour in which he was held by the queen. It is possible that his link with Mortimer, which depends solely on Howel ap Gruffydd's testimony, was through Isabelle, but he had also been involved in rebellion against Edward II, for his lands in Ireland are recorded to have been restored early in 1327. This was the time when the contrariants were coming back into their own. A William Ockley, though not necessarily our man, because variations of the name, such as Ocle, Oakley, were common, was at Southampton in 1322 with Joan, the wife of Roger Mortimer. Mortimer, as may be remembered, had been incarcerated in the Tower and Ockley was one of the custodians of his wife.

Summing up

All our suspects, then, had motive enough to dislike Edward II, but not necessarily to go to the extent of murdering him. In fairness, I think that we must ignore Baker and others following him, and totally exonerate Bishop Orleton, at the same time delivering a not proven verdict in Isabelle's case. If Mortimer did send the fateful letter from Abergavenny, as Howel ap Gruffydd claimed, then the fact might easily have been concealed from the queen. Whatever were Isabelle's feelings for her husband at this stage she could well have realised that his murder would be politically inexpedient. With the murder the fall of the regime of Isabelle and her lover became only a matter of time. Mortimer may have had no qualms, personal or political, but if he were ultimately the guilty party then he has shown himself a deft coverer of his tracks. We know from the manner in which Edward was removed from the kingship that Mortimer had already demonstrated his considerable skill as a political woodsman. His influence was paramount but it was not immediately evident. His will might have been behind the deed and for obvious reasons his instructions could have been verbal.

And so we come to the most likely perpetrators of the deed itself, those gathered at Berkeley. That they acted in anticipation of the expressed wish of their political superiors is possible, but scarcely likely. If they did so, then the crime must be laid at the door of Berkeley and Maltravers, who could certainly have prevented it. Our chief suspect at this local level is Lord Berkeley even if, as Murimuth thought, he and his brother-in-law took monthly turns at guarding the royal prisoner. It was his castle, what went on there was his responsibility. He was, moreover, a more substantial baron in terms of wealth, influence and authority than Maltravers. He was clearly guilty of lying. Though that does not of itself make him a murderer, it does give rise to a measure of suspicion. The case of Maltravers is baffling. He is not known to have left the castle at the crucial time and cannot possibly have been ignorant of what took place right under his nose, yet he was never indicted on the charge of Edward's murder. This leaves Gurney and Ockley as the most likely killers, with the help, connivance or knowledge of Maltravers and possibly of Berkeley as well. If we give credence to the Howel ap Gruffydd story then Ockley had his instructions by word of mouth and by letter at Abergavenny. Both he and Gurney were convicted, but both initially got safely away. Do we need to look any further?

There is a residual niggling doubt. Could it be that there was good reason for the king's failure to secure the summary conviction of Berkeley and Maltravers for negligence so gross as to amount to complicity in the crime? True, he pursued Gurney with great tenacity, but he seems to have held no animosity against the knight's family. In 1331 his widow, Joan, was permitted to farm her deceased husband's Somersetshire manors of Englishcombe (Inglescombe) and Farrington, and their eldest son, another Thomas, was able to petition, successfully it would seem, for the restoration of his lands on achieving his majority. Their third son, Matthew, forged a successful military career, fighting on the continent with Edward III and the Black Prince. Consequently, various historians, not to mention certain chroniclers of the time, have been struck by this apparent anomaly and have even criticised Edward III for what has the look of an inappropriate leniency towards persons in high places. Did Edward III know something that we do not? Did his anxiety to secure the person of Gurney stem, not from the belief that he was a murderer, but from a conviction that he could explain the mysterious happenings at Berkeley?

CHAPTER 7

Hunting Down the Culprits

Extracts from a letter sent to Hudson Gurney Esq. F.R.S., V.P., by the Rev. Joseph Hunter, F. S. A., Torrington Square, November 20 1837.

Dear Sir,

Among the ancient compotuses in the Exchequer which have been lately brought to light by the exertions of the Honourable Board of Commissioners on the Public Records, are several which related to the measures taken by King Edward the Third to bring to justice Sir Thomas de Gournay, the principal actor, as was alleged, in the murder of his father in Berkeley Castle: and as they place the circumstances of his capture, and his ultimate fate, in a light entirely different from that in which they are placed by the old Chroniclers De la Moor and Walsingham, and by modern historians, who, in addition to the Chronicles have had the benefit of the letters relating to this affair which are printed in the *Foedera*, it has occurred to me, that it might be acceptable to the Society of Antiquaries if I were to lay a summary of the contents of these documents before it.

Such is the narrative of the end of Sir Thomas de Gournay, as collected from evidence which appears to be unquestionable. It will be seen that almost every statement of De la Moor and Walsingham is contradicted by this new evidence: 1st. That the arrest was at Marseilles; 2nd. That he was put to death at sea; and 3rd. That he was put to death under orders from England, lest he should implicate certain great persons in the crime, meaning probably the Bishop of Hereford, if not Queen Isabella herself. The last is a point of no small historical importance. As the narrative now stands, Edward appears to have acted throughout the business with the utmost sincerity and integrity of purpose; and indeed the letter which is published in the *Foedera* respecting the examination of Gournay at Burgos, and the certificate to be made of it with all particulars, whoever they might be that were implicated, under the common seal of the city, ought to have relieved him, in the eyes of modern historians, from the unworthy surmise of the contemporary chronicler, that he sought to suppress evidence by the destruction of the witness. As to Walsingham, he is to be regarded only in the light of one who, in this part of his history, has followed an earlier chronicler who may be presumed to have had excellent means of information. But, one part of De la Moor's narrative thus brought to the test of its agreement with the existing contemporary record being found entirely undeserving of credit, it is impossible to prevent a certain amount of suspicion gathering in the mind respecting other information that was given to him concerning the last years of the life of that unhappy prince, which he has exhibited with so painful a particularity. But ... though not fewer than ten or twelve documents selected from the public records relating to this transaction, are printed in the *Foedera*, they fail to correct the errors of the chroniclers, and in fact perplex where they ought to explain. The effect has been, that by one historian of deserved eminence, their testimony has been entirely disregarded, and he has adhered to the narrative of De la Moor and Walsingham ...

Archaeologia 27 (1838)

Hunting Down the Culprits

*W*ITH MORTIMER REMOVED from the scene and the case for murder established, those responsible for the callous affair had been brought to justice, the underlings at least. Justice had to be seen to be done, even if rather late in the day. We may assume too that the emancipated king had a genuine interest in purging sins of omission forced upon him by his tutelage, which had become increasingly irksome. Now he could discover the truth that had been deliberately hidden from him. As with every change of government, there was probably no shortage of disgruntled talebearers anxious to pay off old scores. In these circumstances it is surprising that the number of new suspects is rather small, perhaps a tribute to the lack of vindictiveness on Edward III's part. We have already to some extent anticipated their pursuit by reviewing the outcome of the proceedings against the chief gaoler, Lord Berkeley. An important aspect of his case is that he did not show the most obvious sign of guilt—flight. Anyone else associated with the affair, who was in a position to do so, put as much distance between himself and retribution as he could.

Once again William Ockley is the most perplexing of our quarries. He fled, presumably abroad, and no further trace of him is to be found. Did he die on the continent? If so, what evidence is there of his pursuit by royal agents? Alternatively, did he conceal himself in Ireland, either immediately or at some later date? Failing new information from the recesses of the public records we must admit to having drawn a blank. That his attachment was considered to be a serious matter is indicated by the price placed on his head: a hundred marks if delivered alive, £40 if dead—a mark being 13s. 4d. and a means of calculation rather than a unit of currency. In Thomas Gurney's case the sums were respectively £100 and the same number of marks, sufficient intimation that he was regarded as the major culprit. But before following Gurney on his final adventure we need to dispose summarily of some other suspects.

Isabelle, despite papal concern for her possible fate, was in fact treated with kindness and respect by her son, who visited her diligently during the remainder of her relatively long life. She was deprived of all political influence, but few other restraints were placed upon her. Contrary to the impression given by the northern chronicle which takes its name from Lanercost Priory, she enjoyed a more than adequate income from property, even though initially, in December 1330, she was constrained to surrender all the lands held in dower by her husband's assignment as well as those she had received in abundance in the name of her son. Doubtless she lived a life not dissimilar to that of any other dowager queen before or after her time. Mortimer, we have seen, paid the ultimate penalty for his part, whatever that may have been, in the royal death, and for a whole catalogue of other crimes, some of them capital. Among those condemned with him were Simon de Bereford or Barford and Bogo of Bayeux, or possibly Bayonne since the spelling varies in the documents. Neither of these men is specifically accused of Edward's death, merely of an overall involvement in Mortimer's misdeeds. So far as the rolls of parliament are concerned Mortimer, Gurney and Ockley were the only men convicted of the former king's death.

Baker is the sole chronicler of the time who waxes eloquent on the topic of Gurney's flight. According to him those 'traitorous servants', Gurney and Maltravers, were outlawed owing to the persecution of Queen Isabelle and Bishop Orleton—an obsession of his that we can safely ignore. After three years, Baker continues, Gurney was captured at Marseilles and while being escorted back to England was decapitated at sea for fear he would incriminate certain great prelates and others of the realm. Once again this chronicler is sadly adrift from the facts, but his ideas were committed to posterity by a greater chronicler than he, Thomas Walsingham of the eminent Benedictine monastery of St Albans. What then did happen to Gurney? It is a complicated story.

If the industrious and usually accurate John Smyth is right, Lord Berkeley was guilty of shielding Gurney once it was seen that the axe was literally about to fall—that is after the coup d'état of 19 October 1330 at Nottingham Castle. Gurney presumably was well under cover before parliament assembled in late November, for its intentions could readily be divined. Quite when he left the country is uncertain, but it was presumably after 3 December when

writs were issued to prevent his passage and that of other felons
from the ports, but well before 5 June of the following year
when a commission of enquiry was launched on the report that
two Cornishmen and their accomplices in the coastal village of
Mousehole had assisted Gurney and Maltravers to escape over-
seas, supplying them with armour and necessary provisions.

In the meantime the goods and chattels of Gurney and others
associated with him as 'adherents of Mortimer' were seized by
sheriffs and bailiffs wherever they could be found. In particular
we know of a 'chest and certain casks' which Gurney, then
constable of Bristol, had sent for safekeeping to Keynsham Abbey
nearby. Religious houses were regularly used as safe deposits in
this way, but ecclesiastical censure was powerless against the
immediacy of royal wrath. Directions were given for the opening
of the containers and the sale of their contents under the oversight
of the mayor of Bristol. It could have been early in May of 1331
that Gurney's presence in Spain permeated to English officialdom.
On 23 June the exchequer was ordered to pay £50 to a Ferandus
Ivayns de Greynoun for his passage to and from England. He
had carried news of Gurney's apprehension. Armed with this
information the king had decided to bring the matter to the
attention of his brother monarch of Castile, Alfonso XI, through
formal diplomatic channels. Sir Thomas Gurney, he wrote, a man
accused of the late king's death and in flight from justice, had
been arrested at Burgos and was in a prison within his jurisdiction;
he would like to have him delivered to John de Haustede, the
seneschal of Gascony. Another letter, this time to the mayor and
town officials of Burgos, repeated the request. Just over a week
later, 28 May 1331, Edward wrote again to the Spanish king and
to Burgos reiterating his petition. This time he also asked that
Gurney be examined on the charges against him in the presence
of Bernard Pelegrym or Pilgrim, the royal sergeant-at-arms
who was being sent for the purpose. The prisoner's deposition
or confession was to be appropriately recorded in a notarial
document under the city's seal. If Gurney ever made such a
deposition its survival would be of first-rate importance for our
present enquiry. Once again the records are silent when we
need them most. Edward also invoked the assistance of Alfonso's

chamberlain. This time he asked for Gurney's delivery to the city of Bayonne, where he could await the directions of the king's 'valet' or squire, Giles of Spain. This name we can recognise for he appears among the list of those who surrendered at Caerphilly in 1327. Hence we can assume he was chosen for his likely concern in the affair as a man loyal to Edward II.

Giles of Spain was with Edward III at Bury St Edmunds on 31 May 1331. His expense account provides details of his subsequent movements in pursuit of the fugitive Gurney. He left England on 11 June by the regular route to Wissant in the Pas de Calais. From there he travelled to Paris, where he awaited the arrival of a letter from the king of Castile before resuming the journey to Bordeaux in English Gascony. Leaving that town he sought an interview with the king of Navarre. At this moment we gather there was a hitch in the arrangements for Gurney's handover, a difficulty which sent Giles to Vittoria with Edward III's letter promising £300 to John Martyn de Leyna, the Castilian chamberlain, on surrender of the wanted man. He retraced his steps to Burgos, but finding no solution to the problem set out in pursuit of the king, eventually catching up with him at Madrid, whence he accompanied the court of Segovia. In this manner the autumn and most of the winter were frittered away without tangible result.

At this juncture a confusion arose. A mandate of 13 February 1332 addressed by Edward III to the city of Bayonne urged the authorities there to assist Peter Bernard, another sergeant-at-arms, in the transfer of Gurney 'now under care in your prison' (*iam penes vos carcerali custodia existentem*). In fact, whatever promise had been made, Gurney had not arrived at Bayonne. Giles nonetheless made the journey from Valladodid to Bordeaux to collect the £300 payable in that event, but on his return to Spain found that Gurney had made good his escape. Fruitless enquiries were made in neighbouring Aragon before Giles returned to Burgos to gather details of the getaway. As consolation he gained possession of two other persons, John Tilly and Robert Lynel, who are described in vague terms as 'enemies of the king'. Back in England in the summer after the conclusion of his unsuccessful mission, Giles seems to have engaged in something of a witch-hunt. At

Rochester he arrested William de Kingsclere, near Northampton Sir Richard de Well, and early in 1333, one John le Spicer, all of whom were alleged in some unspecified way to have been implicated in Edward of Caernarvon's death.

Later in 1333 Giles of Spain returned to the continent, wandered about France, and re-entered Spain for a second arrest of Tilly, Gurney's valet or squire, who had either escaped or been released by the authorities. Meanwhile, it had been learned in England that Gurney had reached Naples. In January 1333 his apprehension was entrusted to a Yorkshire knight, Sir William de Thweng. His expense account shows that he left from Dover and travelled to Nice, apparently overland. At Nice he secured a ship to take him to the port of Pisa. From there he travelled the short distance to the city itself, situated a little way from the mouth of the River Arno, and so on to Naples by road. This time there were no difficulties. The fugitive was already in the hands of one of the king's agents, William of Cornwall, for whom Thweng brought some armour. At this stage the expense account shows payments for clothes, linen, shoes and a prison bed for the captive Gurney.

The substantial sum of 400 florins was needed to charter a ship to take Gurney and his escort to Aigues-Mortes, the walled town from which St Louis had embarked for his crusades. If they stopped there it was not for long, since they were shortly at Couloure near Perpignan making arrangements to continue by road. But ill-luck, at any rate from Thweng's point of view, intervened to halt the party's progress. A local family, subjects of the king of Aragon, seems to have had all of them arrested on the grounds of losses formerly suffered at sea by the hands of the English. At some stage they were freed at the intervention of King Alfonso IV, for which Edward, in a letter of October 1333, warmly thanked him. This problem, it would appear, forced Thweng to make a detour through Catalonia. But when the party eventually reached 'Mount Blaunk', a small place near Tarragona, Gurney fell ill and physicians had to be called in to prescribe medicine for his recovery. The journey through Aragon and over the Pyrenees was then resumed, the final stage being by boat down-river to Bayonne. There the physicians had once again to be called to the ailing captive. Their ministrations were of no avail; Sir

Thomas Gurney, doubtless worn out by physical exertion and mental anxiety, died.

That, however, was not the end of the matter. A ship was chartered to transport the body to Bordeaux, some distance to the north, where it was duly 'prepared' or embalmed. Notaries were brought to testify to the circumstances of death; an indication of anxiety to satisfy the king that neither negligence nor criminal act had deprived him of his prey. The party then re-embarked with the corpse for England. The ship put in at Sandwich and then sailed to Tynemouth. Edward III was at Berwick anticipating the surrender of the town by the Scots when Thweng arrived on 7 July 1333. The total cost of Thweng's mission, his own expenses that is, had been just over £350. Gurney's body meanwhile remained on board ship. It was doubtless gibbeted in due course, which might explain the beheading that Baker records. Whether the relatives eventually secured it for Christian burial we have no means of knowing. At least Edward had achieved his purpose, Gurney had been taken 'alive or dead', but one suspects that the king would have preferred the former.

There was a slightly bizarre juxtaposition of events. Shortly before Thweng's arrival at Tynemouth on 26 June Edward had announced that the anniversary of his father, the noble Prince Edward, formerly king of England, whom God assoil, would be kept on the feast of the Translation of St Thomas of Canterbury (3 July) with due solemnity. As for Gurney, the author of the *Scalacronica* records that he had made the name so infamous that an unfortunate squire who bore it was killed in about the year 1334 (he gives no specific date) because of a too ready association with Edward of Caernarvon's murderer. It has been assumed that this unfortunate was the son of the 'regicide', another Thomas, and supposedly father of the Thomas (3) on the Gurney family tree. There is no evidence for the existence of such a man. Thomas (3) was undoubtedly the son of the alleged regicide. The date of his death is unknown, but it was later than 1340. Yet another mystery.

But let us retrace our steps. There is a postscript to Gurney's story which if taken at face value would serve to support the discredited chroniclers against the unvarnished matter-of-fact expense account we have been following. This derives from a French version of the *Brut* chronicles—one of the manuscripts of Corpus Christi College, Oxford. This chronicle not only lends some support to Baker's description of cruelties inflicted on the former king but also puts the full blame for his death, 'the felonious and horrible treason', on Gurney and Maltravers. How the villains were discovered is also explained. Supposedly they were on their way to St James of Compostella in the hope of expiating their crime at the shrine of the saint. It so happened that a certain Isolda de Belhouse was also on pilgrimage. At Burgos, which is certainly on the direct route to Compostella, Isolda took it upon herself to indict the runaways for the royal death. Gurney was clapped in irons and exhibited in the public street, so that everyone could view so dishonourable a traitor. Maltravers eluded pursuit. The Lady Isolda, whose intention to go on pilgrimage is vouched for by the patent rolls, rushed back to England to inform the king, who thereupon, as we have seen, sent someone to apprehend the criminal. At this point the chronicle diverges substantially from the order of events suggested by the expense accounts of Giles of Spain and William de Thweng. The authorities are said to have delivered up their captive, who while under escort escaped to Aragon, where he was recaptured. There is no mention of Naples or of Thweng's separate mission. The anonymous royal envoy (*messager*) is said to have brought his prisoner to Bayonne and left him there while he went to inform the seneschal of Aquitaine, Sir Oliver Ingham. Ingham hastened to Bayonne, fiercely denied hope of pardon to the prisoner, and listened while Gurney openly confessed to the murder and recounted the manner of it. Immediately afterwards Ingham beheaded him and sent the corpse to England.

Now Ingham was a Mortimer supporter and the inference is that he disposed of Gurney to prevent the incrimination of 'certain people' in England. Professor Galbraith seems to have countenanced this version of the story which he himself brought to the light of day. Yet it seems to be as suspect as Baker's chronicle, merely following a common pattern of rumour. Who was Ingham defending? Mortimer was dead, convicted of the crime. It was hardly likely to have been Berkeley, for there is seemingly no evidence for the close association of the two men. Could it have been Queen Isabelle or Adam Orleton? This is scarcely probable, but may indeed be implied after the fashion of Geoffrey le Baker. There is a further question to be asked. Would Ingham have been allowed to get away with taking the law into his own hands in the presence of an agent sent specifically by the king to bring back Gurney, and then boldly suppressing the evidence for purposes of his own? The arm of Edward III was not short, as has been amply demonstrated by the Gurney affair. Are we faced with the usual amalgam of fact and fiction so difficult to disentangle? The manner of Gurney's apprehension is doubtless accurate, the fact that he escaped in Maltravers' company is independently accredited, as we have already noticed, so too is his confession, though in vastly different circumstances; but that he was decapitated alive by Ingham or anyone else may be another manifestation of the common belief that somehow the truth was being hushed up and important persons were being shielded.

Nonetheless, for those who feel reluctant to discard such precautionary decollation there is another theory that can be suggested. We have already encountered John de Haustede as seneschal of Gascony. Haustede's successor, the self-same Sir Oliver Ingham, in July of 1331 received letters of protection for his journey to assume office, at which time the English government believed Gurney to be in custody but not yet extradited. Hence Edward could scarcely have suspected Ingham of harbouring some motive of his own for silencing Gurney. It is conceivable, therefore, that two years later the seneschal acted in his royal master's interest (and on his secret instruction?) to prevent Gurney divulging information which would incriminate Edward's mother, Isabelle. The hypothesis is rather shaky; it may be safer to accept that Gurney's well-attested illness proved fatal without outside intervention and that it was only his corpse that suffered decapitation.

CHAPTER 8

But Did the King Really Die?

Edward of Caernarvon brought to life again 1330

Certain men of this land, to the intent to try what friends they had in England, craftily devised that Edward the Second, king of England, was alive in the castle of Corfe, but not to be seen in the day time, and therefore they used many knights to make shows and masking with dancing upon the towers and walls of the castle. Which being perceived by people of the country, it was thought there had been some great king unto whom they did these great solemnities. This rumour was spread over all England, to wit, that the old king was alive; whence it came to pass that the Earl of Kent sent thither a friar preacher to try the truth of the matter, who (as it is thought) having corrupted the porter of the castle with rewards, is let in, where he lay all day in the porter's lodge very close, and when night was come, he was willed to put on the habit of a layman, and then was brought into the hall, where he saw (as he thought) Edward, the father of the king, sitting royally at supper, with great majesty. This friar, being thus persuaded, returned again to the Earl of Kent and reported, as he thought, what he saw; whereupon the earl said and affirmed with an oath that he would endeavour by all the means he could to deliver his brother from prison.

John Stow, *Annals*, translating Baker's passage in the *Chronicon*. Spelling modernised.

Edmund, Earl of Kent, seeks his brother 1330

And upon a time it befell that Sir Edmund of Woodstock, Earl of Kent, spoke unto the pope John XXII at Avignon, and said that Almighty God had many times done for love of Thomas of Lancaster many great miracles to many men and women that were through diverse sickness undone as to the world and through his prayer they were brought unto their health. And so Sir Edmund prayed the pope heartily that he would grant him grace that the foresaid Thomas might be translated, but the pope said 'Nay, he should not be translated, the same Thomas, Earl of Lancaster, until the time that he were better certified of the clergy of England.'

And when this Edmund saw that he might nought speed of his purpose as touching the translation, he prayed him of his counsel as touching Sir Edward of Caernarvon, his brother, and that not long gone was king of [England], what thing might best be done as touching his deliverance, since that a common fame is throughout England that he was alive, and whole and safe. When the pope heard him tell that Sir Edward was alive, he commanded the earl, upon his benison, that he should help, with all the power that he might, that he were delivered out of prison and save his body in all manner that he might, and for to bring this thing unto an end he assoiled him and his company *a pena et a culpa*, and all those that should help towards his deliverance. Then took Edmund of Woodstock, Earl of Kent, his leave of the pope and came back again into England. And when Edmund was come some of the friars preacher came and said that Sir Edward his brother yet was alive in the castle of Corfe under the keeping of Sir Thomas Gurney. Then sped him the foresaid Edmund as fast as he might, till that he came to the castle of Corfe, and acquainted him and spake him so fair with Sir John Daveril, that was constable of the aforesaid castle, and gave him rich gifts for to have acquaintance of him, and for to know of his counsel, and thus it befell that the aforesaid Sir Edmund prayed specially for to tell him privily of his brother, Sir Edward, if that he lived or were dead. If that he were alive, he prayed of him once to have a sight. And this John Daveril was a high-hearted man, and full of courage and answered shortly that Sir Edward his brother was in health and under his keeping and dared show him unto no man since it was defended him in the king's behalf, Edward, that was Edward son of Caernarvon, and also through commandment of the queen Isabelle, the king's mother, and of Sir Roger the Mortimer, that he should show his body to no man of the world, save only unto him, upon pain of life and limb ... but the false traitor lied, for he was not in his ward, but he was taken thence, and led to the castle of Berkeley through Sir Thomas Gurney, through commandment of the Mortimer, till that he was dead ... But Sir Edmund of Woodstock wist nothing that his brother was dead. Whereupon he took a letter unto the foresaid Sir John and prayed him heartily that he would take it to King Edward his brother as his worthy lord.

English *Brut* (anonymous) chronicle. Edited F. W. D. Brie, Early English Text Society. Slightly adapted and with modernised spelling.

But did the King Really Die?

*W*E HAVE NOW CONCLUDED our examination of the mysterious death of Edward II, tried our hand at gauging the culpability of no more than a handful of available suspects, three of whom were convicted of the crime, two of them *in absentia*. Expectedly the political responsiblity for Edward's death has been laid on Mortimer without opportunity to reply—a right which the law of the time allowed him. The rolls of parliament record a petition for the *post mortem* rehabilitation of Edmund of Kent for whose killing the Earl of March in his final moments is said to have admitted his guilt 'before the people'. He did not even then confess to responsibility for Edward's murder.

We have followed the Somersetshire knight, Gurney, in his frenetic attempts to elude his bulldog-like pursuers in Spain and Italy. Some may even have been persuaded that the vigorous and expensive series of operations launched against the fugitive prove that Edward III felt him to be the most guilty of all his suspects, the man who actually perpetrated the deed. Yet as early as 1331 his widow Joan was permitted to farm some of his lands at Englishcombe and Farrington in Somerset and, on coming of age eight years later, his eldest son Thomas successfully petitioned for restoration of his estates. Another son, Matthew, was to become a celebrated warrior in the armies of Edward III and the Black Prince. Moreover, in the course of our investigation we were tempted to concede that there was something suspicious about the manner in which the two principal gaolers, Maltravers and Berkeley, were not convicted, at the very least of being accessories.

We now come to the most baffling of all the documents we have encountered thus far. If it is genuine, or to be more exact, the copy of a genuine original, then we shall have to reject virtually all that we have provisionally accepted, leastways with respect to guilt. This document, couched in the form of the personal confession of Edward of Caernarvon, assures us that the 'victim' did not in fact die at Berkeley in or about 21 September 1327, nor was he buried at Gloucester in the magnificent tomb which was shortly to be built for the reception of his body. Instead, he escaped, wandered about the continent in the guise of a pilgrim, visited the pope in Avignon, became an assiduous hermit in Lombardy, and finally left his bones in an alien abbey, at any rate until they were abstracted in the time-honoured tradition of mediaeval relic snatching. Better still, this is no anonymous document, a man of substance has appended his name to it, and it is directed to none other than Edward III himself, but without an initial address clause. It is not dated though, which must be accounted a serious oversight.

Before examining the provenance of the document and the *bona fides* of its reputed author, as also some other evidence in its support, we had better study a text rendered in English out of the Italianate Latin in which it is written. I have taken the precaution of rendering the place-names and some other words as they appear in the document to give some sense of its foreign flavour.

The Fieschi Letter

In the name of the Lord, Amen. Those things which I have heard from your father's confession I have written down with my own hand and I have further taken pains that they should be made known to your lordship. First of all he says that feeling that there was subversion against him in England and, moreover, warned by your mother, he left his retinue in the castle of the Earl Marshal by the sea called Chepstow (*Gesosta*). Afterwards, under the influence of fear, he embarked on a boat (*barcham*) with (*con*) the lords Hugh Despenser, the Earl of Arundel, and some others, and landed in Glamorgan by sea,* and there was captured, together with (*con*) the said Hugh and M. Robert de Baldock (*Baldoli*). They were captured by the lord Henry of Lancaster (*de Longo Castello*), who led him to the castle of Kenilworth (*Chilongarda*), while others were taken to various places. There he lost his crown at the insistence of many persons. Afterwards you were crowned at the following feast of St Mary, Candlemas (*le Candelor*). Eventually they sent him to the castle of Berkeley (*Berchele*). Afterwards the servant

---

* Edward was at Chepstow 18–19 October 1326, at sea on the 20th, at Cardiff on the 25th.

that kept watch over him, when some time [had elapsed], said to your father: 'Lord, the lord Thomas de Gornay and the lord Symon Bereford (*Desberfort*), knights, have come to kill you. If you wish, I will give you my clothes (*raubas*) so that you can the more easily escape.' Then with these clothes, at twilight (*hora quasi noctis*), he left the prison. And when he had reached the last gate without resistance, because he was not recognised, he found the gatekeeper asleep. He at once killed him, and having taken the keys of the door, he opened it and escaped, together with the warder who was guarding him. The aforesaid knights who came to kill him, seeing that he had escaped in this manner, and fearing the queen's wrath, even more the danger to their own persons, after removing his heart placed the above mentioned porter (*portarium*) in a container (*cusia*) and maliciously presented the heart and body of the said porter to the queen, so that the porter was buried as the body of the king in Gloucester (*Glocesta'*). And after he had gone from the dungeons (*carceres*) of the aforesaid castle, he was received in Corfe Castle (*Corf*) with (*con*) his companion who had guarded him in the dungeons by the lord Thomas castellan of the said castle, unknown to the lord John Maltravers (*Maltraverse*), lord of the said Thomas. In that castle he remained secretly for a year and a half. Then, having heard that the Earl of Kent was beheaded, because he had said that he [Edward] was alive, he boarded a ship with the same custodian, and with the consent of the said Thomas, who had received him, crossed over to Ireland (*Yrlandam*), where he remained for nine months. After that, fearing that he should be recognised there, having assumed the habit of a hermit (*habitu unius hermite*) he returned to England, landed at the port of Sandwich, and in the same habit crossed the sea to Sluys (*apud Sclusam*). Then he made his way to Normandy, and from Normandy to many other places, and crossing Languedoc (*per Linguam Octanum*) came to Avignon where, after giving a florin to the pope's servant, sent by his means a written message (*cedula*) to the pope, John [XXII]. The pope summoned him to his audience (*ad se*) and secretly kept him with honour for more than fifteen days. Finally, after various discussions and much consideration, armed with a licence he went to Paris, from Paris to Brabant (*Braybantia'*), from Brabant to Cologne out of devotion to see [the shrine of] the three kings, and leaving Cologne he crossed by way of Germany, that is to say made his journey, by Milan into Lombardy and from Milan entered a hermitage in the castle of Melazzo (*Milasci*). He stayed in that hermitage for two and a half years, but because war enveloped the castle, he transferred himself to the castle of Cecima (*Cecime*), another hermitage within the diocese of Pavia (*Papiensis*) in Lombardy. He was in this last hermitage for two years, or thereabouts, always enclosed, doing penance, and praying for you and other sinners. In testimony whereof I have had a seal appended for your Highness' consideration.

Your Manuele Fieschi (*de Flisco*), notary of the lord pope, your devoted servant.

For a papal notary the Latin appears more than a little halting, not to say repetitive, but that could be a subjective observation. One authority has claimed that the orthography, strange as it is, is to be found in Genoese documents of that time. The gist of the story is clear enough and there is a noticeable attention to precise detail, even where this is not really significant—the 'more than fifteen days' stay at Avignon, for instance. This might be expected in an attempt to discredit the generally held opinion that the former king had died. Another point to be made at the outset is the gross impropriety of the overt revelation of the secrets of the confessional, something which has been largely glossed over. Bishop Orleton when accused of treasonable converse with his 'parishioner', Mortimer, at the time of the 1321–1322 rebellion was adamant that he would say nothing of what he had learned by virtue of his pastoral office. Next, chronology is important if authenticity, or its reverse, is to be established. Some preliminary remarks may help here. One obvious error has been glossed over by previous commentators. If Edward had stayed at Corfe for only one and a half years after 21 September 1327, or thereabouts, he would not have been in a position to learn of Kent's beheading on 19 March 1330. Two and a half years is the required interval. There is no suggestion that Edward wandered about the countryside before being admitted to Corfe. That would scarcely have been possible in view of the likely hue and cry. If we take that to be

a slip* then rather more than nine months after Kent's death
Edward touched at (*applicuit*) Sandwich—apparently he did not
go by land through England, which certainly would have been
dangerous—and then crossed to Sluys. That would indicate a
time early in 1331, not the best of seasons for travelling. The only
other element that can be dated from 'internal evidence', that
provided by the document itself, is the visit to the pope. We
know John XXII died 4 December 1334, so the pilgrim would
need to have reached his court at Avignon by November of that
year at the very latest, in order to allow for a fortnight's stay.

Now the letter-writer himself, Manuele de Fieschi, requires
investigation. He was a scion of that prolific ecclesiastical family
centred on Genoa, which is said to have produced in its time two
popes, Innocent IV and Adrian V, seventy-two cardinals, and a
hundred bishops. Thus, unlike some of the authors of suspect
letters or documents which have already been examined, he is no
nonentity, nor is there any obvious reason why he should have
had an axe to grind in the turmoil of English political life. As was
common enough for a mediaeval cleric with a Western European
perspective, he did have some English benefices. In 1329 he became
a canon of Salisbury and also archdeacon of Nottingham in the
diocese of Lincoln. A relative of his, Nicolino de Fieschi, termed
the 'cardinal of Genoa', was in 1336 successfully negotiating on
behalf of his compatriots for compensation for one of their plun-
dered galleys. This was one of the ships attacked by the exiled
younger Despenser off the dunes near Sandwich. Edward III, while
denying his father's complicity, found it prudent, no doubt
because of his interest in the Genoese as shipbuilders and potential
suppliers of vessels against the French, to come to an amicable
settlement. This he did, but at the heavy cost of eight thousand
marks. Another of the Fieschi clan, Carlo, had been a member of
Edward II's council and was regarded by him as a (distant) relative

---

* A modern forgery might well have confused the issue in this respect
  since 19 March 1329 would be the 'old style' date for Kent's death,
  the year 1330 commencing on 25 March. The interval, of course,
  remains the same.

(*consanguineus*). Thus it would seem that the *bona fides* of Manuele is beyond question.

Where does the document come from? It was discovered by Alexandre Germain in a cartulary of Gaucelme de Deaux, Bishop of Maguelonne, which was allegedly compiled in 1368. Maguelonne, an important place in the Middle Ages, was to be largely destroyed by Louis XIII in 1633. It is now a hamlet bordered by the Mediterranean and commanded by its mediaeval church. The surviving records are housed in the *Archives départmentales* of Hérault at Montpellier. One writer comments that the document was 'inserted haphazard amongst a lot of feudal documents relating to the barony of Sauve adjudged to the bishops of Maguelonne by Philip *le bel*.' Germain brought his intriguing find to the notice of savants in Paris during 1877 and published it privately the following year. Following its publication (1881) in the transactions of the archaeological society of Montpellier it became fairly widely known, at least among the fraternity of antiquaries. Even before that news of the document had percolated to England where Theodore Bent published it in 1880, both in *Macmillan's Magazine* and in *Notes and Queries*. Sir Henry Ogle, from the Northumbrian branch of that family, referred to it in a paper delivered for him in 1890 at the Society of Antiquaries of Newcastle-on-Tyne. Already, in 1883, Bishop Stubbs had brought the document to the notice of historians by publishing it with comments in his introduction to the 'de la More version' of Baker. In recent years it has been republished at least twice and on each occasion the historian responsible has been unable or unwilling to dismiss it as spurious. In short, it has defied the test of time. Clearly we shall have to take it seriously.

It will be felt immediately that once again a document is striving to convince us by its circumstantial nature. A whole variety of places and incidents is included. Only someone very close to the events could have known about some of them. It may even be conceded that it has more of the ring of truth than some of the writing of contemporary chroniclers, notably Baker. How accurate is it then by the yardstick of the 'facts' as we know them, or to put it another way, what holes can be picked in it?

First of all, there is an almost uncanny accuracy about that part of the Fieschi letter which takes us as far as the burial (of a porter's body?) at Gloucester. We have the well-attested escape by sea to Glamorgan, the capture by Henry of Lancaster, and almost incredibly, the story of the heart being sent to Isabelle, though clearly the body never was, but that can be taken as a bit of shorthand, as it were. Then there is the date, Candlemass, given for Edward III's coronation. At least one distinguished mediaeval historian and a notable encyclopaedia have dated the coronation 29 January. In fact it took place during the Candlemass festival, as the document states, though the feast itself fell on Monday in 1327, rather than on the Sunday of the coronation, the eve of Candlemass.

It will be noticed at once that another name is added to our list of criminals. A Simon de Bereford is said to have come with Gurney to kill Edward. Now Bereford had been one of the most dedicated of Mortimer supporters. He came from Leicestershire where his lands were confiscated on account of his rebellion against the king. In 1327 not only were these lands restored, for his services to Isabelle he was also granted a manor in Chesham, Buckinghamshire, together with another, Fritheby, in Leicestershire, which had belonged to Despenser. At the time he is recorded to have held property elsewhere as well, some of it possibly of recent acquisition. He also enjoyed what was doubtless the fairly lucrative position of royal escheator for the lands south of the River Trent. Here was a man who had everything to lose if Mortimer fell. When the blow came he was one of those condemned for complicity in the earl's misdeeds. He had already made preparations for escape abroad by leaving valuables worth two thousand pounds in the care of the prior of Tackley at the latter's house in Cripplegate, London. Prompt action of the authorities prevented his escape and he was among those hanged by parliamentary decree. It will be noted, nonetheless, that the parliamentary record does not specifically convict him of Edward's death.

There is another difficulty apart from the chronological problem arising from the length of Edward's stay at Corfe. Lord Maltravers certainly held considerable property in Dorset, the county in which Corfe lies, but the constable of the castle at the time was unquestionably Sir John Deveril, of whom more will be learned in

connection with his deceitful activities there. At the same time the
Berkeley accounts reveal that Maltravers was certainly at Corfe
for an undefined period and that he was paid £258 8s. 2d. for
expenses of the king's father in Dorset. Moreover, some letters
were sent to him there. It is sufficient to state here that Maltravers
was no friend of Edward's and that he would surely have learned
of any arrangements going on behind his back. Who then was the
inadequately described 'Thomas', the abettor and concealer of the
fugitive? We just do not know. Could the name represent some
confusion with Gurney? One popular chronicler says he was there
as Edward's gaoler. Bearing in mind the seeming authenticity of
the rest of the document such a confusion, if such it is, appears
out of character.

Once the Fieschi letter transports our quarry to the mists of
Ireland we have no means of checking the 'facts'. Later on we
have to take account of some very questionable, not to say fan-
tastic, interpretations by Italian investigators, which have not been
accepted by the standard works of reference in their country—
which is not surprising. Here we must acknowledge a considerable
debt to the material and discussion made available in the journal
Speculum by Professor Cuttino, though our criticism of some aspects of this 'evidence' may turn out to be more forthright. The
two places in Lombardy where Edward is said by the Fieschi letter
to have stayed were first 'positively identified' by Anna Benedetti,
a professor from Palermo, in her book about Edward's connection
with Italy which was published in 1924. They are Cecima sopra
Voghera and the abbey of Sant' Alberto di Butrio. This is not un-
convincing, unlike some of the good professor's further
deductions, which betray an astonishing gullibility. Only a
minimum training in iconography and architectural history would
be required to appreciate that the historiated Romanesque capitals
at the abbey could not have been carved in the fourteenth century,
save by some master-faker, hence they cannot be given allegorical
significance for the events taking place at that time in England.
They do not, in other words, provide a veiled interpretation in
stone of Edward's oppression and death.

A plaque in the abbey, which for the most part relies heavily
on information from the Fieschi letter, adds something not stated

there—that the bones of the king-hermit were stolen, carried to England, and there placed in the tomb at Gloucester by Edward III. Where, one wonders, did this story come from? Yet, if we accept the premise that Edward was indeed buried in the Italian abbey in a tomb (now empty) adjacent to the cloister, it would have been essential, once this fact became known, to have at least some of the remains transported to Gloucester so that the veneration taking place there would have appropriate authenticity. Must we envisage Edward III's agents tracking down relics as well as criminals?

The tradition, of indeterminate date, is that the abbey of Sant' Alberto once housed the corpse of Edward II. If we are tempted to be sceptical, as might well be the case, preferring to attribute the 'legend' to the Fieschi letter, then we have to contend with the statement by one Domenico Sparpaglione—given some countenance by Professor Cuttino—that in 1958 a man of 88 remembered the story told by his grandfather of an English king (not specifically Edward) who had been a hermit at Sant' Alberto. That would take the 'memory' well back beyond 1900. Since the Fieschi letter was not *widely* known in Italy until well after that time—or so it is said—there must be an independent folk tradition to be reckoned with. The case is not quite watertight, since independent enquiry could have been undertaken any time after the initial discovery of the Fieschi letter. Local peasants might indeed recall the rudiments of the story, even if the circumstances of how it came into their heads were forgotten. On the whole the support of a folk memory based on one elder's recollection is at best somewhat nebulous.

If that line of corroboration be discarded, another has been advanced, this time with specific reference to the chronology of Fieschi's own movements. Assuming that Manuele left England about 1336, as does Professor Cuttino, for business on the continent, he could have penned the original letter, incorporating Edward's confession, any time thereafter until shortly before 6 July 1343. At the latter date Fieschi became Bishop of Vercelli, which means that he would not have described himself in the valedictory phrase at the close of the letter as notary public of the pope. Instead he would have adopted a style more in keeping with his new dignity. Now the earlier of these dates is just three years after Gurney's death and one year before Berkeley's apparently undeserved final acquittal. The later date, 1343, is precisely two years before Edward III's softening of his attitude towards Maltravers, which resulted in the grant to him of letters of protection so that he could set about the process of clearing his name. Could it be that learning of the confession Edward III at last realised that neither Gurney nor Maltravers was guilty of the death of his father after all? Could Gurney's much sought after confession, presuming he was well enough to make it, have been to the effect that his offence was not the murder of his captive but the palming off of a commoner's body for the royal corpse? All this must remain in the realm of conjecture. But there is another point. If Gurney was considered by Edward III to be guilty of so heinous a crime, why was it that as early as 1331 not only was his widow allowed to farm his lands at Englishcombe and elsewhere but also, that when her son Thomas came of age early in 1340, his inheritance was restored to him promptly and without question?

Before leaving this matter a suggestion might be made. The earlier date, 1336, given for Fieschi's departure from England, could be pushed back a little. The Salisbury records indicate that Canon Fieschi was abroad in September 1333, when the chapter wrote requesting his assistance at the curia or papal court. Admittedly letters were issued on his behalf in both December 1333, for one year, and again in June 1335, for two, which permitted him to appoint attorneys to act in his interests while absent, but there is no evidence that he actually returned in the interval. The earlier date would be preferable from the standpoint of Edward the hermit's itinerary, since he could then have reached Avignon and made his confession by 1332, or at any rate 1333, much more feasible dates.

Even were this argument to be dismissed as being somewhat too speculative, we would need to take account of two apparently confirmatory items of evidence. The first of these is rather easier to deal with than the second. Murimuth and Baker, despite a confusion as to chronology, and also the English *Brut* chronicle, combine in support of the notion that Edward of Caernarvon was at some time or other at Corfe, and this is corroborated by entries in the Berkeley accounts mentioned above in connection with Maltravers. Why was he taken there? A letter has survived among the so-called 'Ancient Correspondence' in the Public Record Office that gives good reason for his temporary removal from Berkeley. According to Professor Tanquerey its author was John Walwayn, a clerk who had seen lengthy royal service and possibly the younger brother of his namesake, the putative author of the *Vita Edwardi Secundi*, from which we have occasion to quote. This attribution has been shown to be erroneous, being derived from a calendaring error. The real author of the letter—which is dated 27 July 1327—was in fact Berkeley himself. He was writing to warn the chancellor, John Hothum, Bishop of Ely, of a conspiracy involving persons from Staffordshire, Warwickshire and Glouces-tershire. The conspirators' aim was to rescue the king. The letter also draws attention to a remote uprising developing in Bucking-hamshire, of which Berkeley had been told by members of his household. The more immediate threat was posed by the maraud-ing band led by the brothers Thomas and Stephen Dunheved, whose activities have earlier attracted our attention. It might be thought strange that these 'rioters', as the authorities dubbed them, exhibit a strong ecclesiastical connection, but that merely indicates the degree of popular clerical support for the deposed king, particularly among the friars. There were two friars apart from Thomas Dunheved, one of them like himself a Dominican, as well as a Cistercian monk from Hailes Abbey near Winchcomb, and an Augustinian canon of Llanthony, Edward's resting place en route to Berkeley.

Lord Berkeley, who despite the emergency seems to have been a stickler for the regulations, complained that his commission was insufficient to permit him to deal with those involved, which is why in the following month he was specifically empowered to do so. But the really striking information comes at the commencement of the letter. It is to the effect that the former king had been taken from Berkeley and the castle itself sacked. Lord Berkeley's com-mission cites the plundering of the castle, but seemingly judiciously omits mention of the captive's escape. However, a mandate to the sheriff of Oxfordshire, dated 20 August 1327, records the indictment before Lord Berkeley as keeper of the king's peace in Gloucestershire of one William de Aylemere—two rectors of this name are listed in an earlier indictment. This time the charge was one of consenting to and abetting the plundering of Berkeley Castle, the abducting of Edward of Caernarvon, and the raising of the populace in war against the king. Aylemere was to be released from Oxford gaol if he could find adequate sureties for his production in court. Once again these constitute isolated fragments of information. We are not told whether Edward was recaptured at this particular time or later, perhaps not at all! There is scant indication of the means adopted to recover the fugitive, merely an indictment of rioters, who were common enough at this period and many of whom had earlier been indicted for a variety of felonies. At least we learn that Edward was taken from captivity.

The next fragment of evidence is of an entirely different kind, comprising two entries in a wardrobe book, in which was kept the record of minor royal expenses. Edward III, in pursuance at the outbreak of the Hundred Years War of his alliance with the Emperor Louis or Lewis IV, travelled to Coblence for his ceremonial investment as vicar of the Empire. Whilst there a certain William le Galeys, 'the Welshman', was arrested at nearby Cologne. A royal sergeant-at-arms, Francis Lumbard, escorted him to the king. What happened at this meeting we are not told, indeed we would hardly expect to come by such details in the laconic entries of a wardrobe book. What we do learn is that at Antwerp, the royal base on the continent, a Francekins Forcet claimed expenses for Galeys' custody for three weeks of December 1338. Apparently the prisoner had been taken to Antwerp after his interview. He then vanishes from history; one hopes not from life itself. The entries containing these tantalising titbits of information are separated in the wardrobe book. In the first Galeys is said to have claimed to be the king's father, in the second to have called himself the king of England, father of the present king—though those words may only be the approximations of the scribe concerned. Can this be regarded as providing confirmation of the 'real Edward' and his presence as a pilgrim in Cologne? Probably not. The date is somewhat late, since it would presuppose an excessively long period of peregrination after the stay at Avignon.

There remains the possibility that this piece of 'real history' could have provided a useful circumstance for the fabricator, if there was such a person. Clearly if the Fieschi letter is not genuine then it has to include as many verifiable facts or near facts as possible in order to sustain verisimilitude.

Recently yet another extraordinary coincidence has been brought to my attention. In May 1332 Eleanor, Edward II's daughter, was married at Nijmegen to Reginald, Count of Guelders (Guelderland). A detailed expense account of the time reveals that a 'Willelmus de Cornevill', described as 'valet de chambre' (*valettus de camera*) of Eleanor was allowed expenses for a journey to Cologne to the shrine of the three kings. Can he be identified as that William of Cornwall whom we have encountered as the capturer of Thomas Gurney? Are we to assume that he is going on his own or is he accompanying someone at the behest of his mistress? If the latter, who can this be? Edward of Caernarvon, a clandestine figure at his daughter's marriage? A tempting hypothesis, and the date is not unhelpful, though it does not coincide with Galeys' appearance. But there is a danger of piling fantasy upon fantasy and making more of this than we should. Presumably many must have made such a pilgrimage from Brabant. We are on surer ground, however, with the almost equally surprising fact that Manuele de Fieschi became provost of Arnhem in 1332 and could therefore have known about Cornwall's pilgrimage.

Such impersonation was no isolated phenomenon. On the contrary, impersonators of kings were relatively commonplace, not least during Edward II's reign. There was a popular assumption that since no genuine king could be expected to behave in such an unkingly manner, Edward must surely be a changeling. Notions of this kind figure widely in the chronicles; in the *Scalacronica*, the Lanercost chronicle, the Pauline Annals and the *Brut*, to mention only some. In the case of Galeys, though, the point of interest is that by then Edward of Caernarvon was no longer alive, officially at least.

There are two further elements for consideration; both concern the corpse. We know from Murimuth what efforts were made to demonstrate that there had been no foul play. We also know that he expressed doubt about the possibility of taking a close look at the corpse. Could it be that the reason for this was that the body was not Edward's but the porter's? Then again there is the proposition that this was the first *known* occasion that a mannequin was used in Western Europe. Did this also arise from the fact that the body itself had to be kept beyond the range of clear recognition? Those who regard the Fieschi letter as genuine will latch onto these details as tending to confirm their belief.

Summarising our impressions at this stage of the Fieschi letter, we shall find no difficulty in admitting that it is an impressively detailed, circumstantial document. If it be a forgery—and forgeries were far from uncommon in mediaeval times—then it was a fairly convincing one; if not, then we have a suitable explanation for Edward III's conduct towards Maltravers and Berkeley. A note of caution. We have no evidence that the king actually received a letter even though it is ostensibly directed to him. The original has not been found. On this last point it could be argued that, letter or no, if the information it contains is true it could well have been conveyed by word of mouth. It is often forgotten, even by those who ponder so recalcitrant a problem as this one, that the most secret thoughts were regularly conveyed by messenger rather than on paper or more accurately, parchment; a practice which allows room for imaginative reconstruction on the part of historians.

There is a final twist to this tortuous affair. We have spoken without explanation of the Earl of Kent's death and somewhat darkly of Maltravers' 'other crime'. It is time to remove these ambiguities. The fifth of the plethora of charges against Mortimer in 1330 was that, knowing well that the king was dead and buried, he had deceived the Earl of Kent into thinking that he was alive and had him put to death on that account at Winchester. We have not commented upon the fact, but the gist of the matter is included in the Fieschi letter. The manner in which Kent was duped has been described in great detail by the *Brut* chronicler; variations of the story are discoverable in numerous other places.

It would appear from the *Brut* and indeed from the papal records that Edmund, Earl of Kent, did pay a visit to John XXII in order to urge the pope to canonise Thomas of Lancaster, victim of his own truculent nature but also of a temporarily resurgent and ruthless Edward II. Quite why Kent lent himself to such a political manoeuvre is not at all clear, although opposition to the ruling clique was coalescing around the 'martyred' earl's name. The pope was not too well disposed towards the idea and insisted that more adequate documentation of Lancaster's suitability, including one supposes the attested performance of posthumous miracles, should be provided by the ecclesiastical authorities—the appropriate channel of communication. At that point Kent is said to have turned the conversation to another matter, his conviction that his half-brother, Edward the former king, was still alive. Later John XXII was to remark that he had in no way countenanced any such story. It was well known, he stressed, that Edward had died and been publicly buried with due solemnity. Had not the earl himself attended the exequies? Mortimer, however, perhaps uncertain of his own political position, was irritated with Kent for his part in the unsuccessful rebellion of January 1329. Clearly he felt him to be a focus of opposition, imputing to Kent a traitorous association with unnamed enemies at home and abroad. It is doubtful whether Mortimer had any real fear of Kent himself, for the earl was a weak character, easily duped and politically ineffectual. What he intended to do was to flush out the mounting opposition, using the earl as a catspaw.

Agents provocateurs were employed by Mortimer or his agents to entrap the gullible earl and any others who rose to the bait. Maltravers seems to have been close to the centre of this operation with Sir John Deveril, constable of Corfe, as one of his principal agents. To judge from the indictment in the parliament roll of 1330 Simon de Bereford and Bogo of Bayeux or Bayonne also had parts to play in the plot.

One version of the *Brut* chronicle describes how Edmund, Earl of Kent, was lured by certain Dominican friars into the belief that Edward of Caernarvon was a prisoner in Corfe castle. The earl hastened there and tried to persuade John Deveril to let him in. The constable declared that he had been strictly prohibited from giving entry to anyone. Thereupon the earl entrusted him with a letter which Deveril, as soon as the coast was clear, took straight to Mortimer. Baker's account, followed by the Elizabethan Stow in his *Annals*, is even more colourful. According to this version the castle at Corfe became a scene of ostentatious festivity, with torches illuminating the walls and battlements, for the sole purpose of deceiving the credulous in the surrounding countryside. Simultaneously the rumour that the old king remained alive was spread abroad. Hearing this, the Earl of Kent sent a Dominican friar to investigate. The friar had himself concealed in the gatekeeper's room until nightfall when he was allowed into the hall in secular clothing. There a person whom he took to be Edward was seated at a splendid feast. News of this incited Kent to make plans for his brother's release. One wonders, in view of all the contrived rejoicing, why this was thought to be necessary!

The Lanercost chronicler's account is different again. In his story it is the Dominican Thomas Dunheved (in fact considered to have been dead by that time) who came to the earl with the tale that he had raised the devil. The apparition told him that Edward was alive. Subsequently, with three other friars, he urged that the captive be released and restored to the throne. Another version of the *Brut* claims that Gurney was the royal gaoler at Corfe, Deveril being, as elsewhere, the constable.

It will be appreciated from all this that rumours of every kind were rife and imagination given free rein. But if the chroniclers were unduly credulous, what of the many people in high places who became entangled in the plot? Numbered among them were William Melton, the Archbishop of York, Stephen Gravesend, the Bishop of London, the Abbot of Langdon, an old friend of Edward's, various friar provincials and numerous important laymen. Heavy fines, imprisonment or exile followed, but the luckless Kent was summarily executed at the time of the Winchester parliament once someone sufficiently base could be persuaded to perform the deed. Isabelle was supposedly furious at Kent's behaviour and the king, who might well have wished to save his uncle's life, seems to have been deprived of any opportunity to intervene.

It is only too apparent that a number of the Fieschi letter's ingredients are here, but whereas the Italian's letter purports to be true, the entrapment of Kent was engineered by false pretences. The disenchantment of those who wished to keep the memory of Edward green was real enough, but how many seriously believed in Mortimer's fabrication it would be hard to say. Some may have considered the memory of the king to be enough to act as a rallying cry for the disaffected. The ruse was in the main successful, for Mortimer flushed out some of his enemies. The more prudent were content to bide their time—Richard de Bury and William de Montacute, authors of Mortimer's downfall, among them.

Of course, those now convinced of the validity of the Fieschi letter will be able to consider that Kent's insurrection, if such a disorderly charade can be dignified by that name, was based on reality, not fiction, even if the reality was traduced by Mortimer in his own interests. Others may prefer to think that fact and fiction have been kaleidoscoped and that the true picture is gone for ever.

Perpendicular style at Gloucester, 'Crécy' window and retrochoir vault.

*Tomb of Archbishop John
Stratford, Canterbury Cathedral.*

Norman masonry in Englishcombe Church.

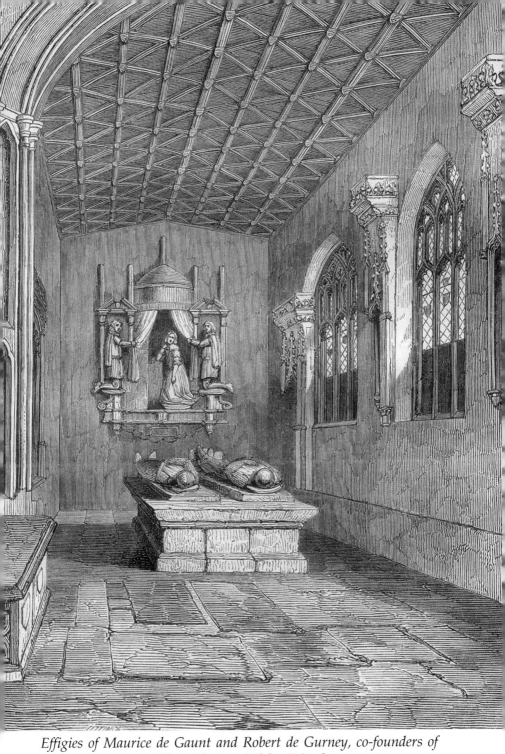

Effigies of Maurice de Gaunt and Robert de Gurney, co-founders of Billeswick Hospital by Bristol.

CHAPTER 9

A Possible Solution?

Isabelle's Reconciliation?

Burial near many loved ones not only promised temporal solace for the remains of those confronting death; it also offered the prospect that, at the resurrection, the different portions of the body would rise with those of relatives and friends to enjoy, with them, the same sort of companionship in heaven that they had on earth.

> E. A. R. Brown, *Death of the Human Body in the Later Middle Ages.*

The Face of Edward II

No one ... can look upon the effigy which lies on the tomb in Gloucester Cathedral without a strong conviction that the face is not merely a sculptor's ideal, nor even a conventional representation of the dead king, but that those chiselled features are the exact form and model of those of Edward of Carnarvon himself. The character and individuality of the head and face are astonishing, and are strongly indicative of such a nature and disposition, weak and self indulgent, yet obstinate, as we know Edward possessed. The large size of the head, the broad, high, and full development of the upper part of the forehead, the utter flatness and deficiency of what are called the perceptive faculties about the region of the eyebrows, the rather small, straight, and pointed nose, the weak, querulous mouth, combine to form a countenance most striking and peculiar— that once seen could never be mistaken or forgotten. That the corpse of the castle porter could ever be exhibited, even partially or superficially, for that of a king with such a presence as this is utterly incredible.

> J. H. Cooke F. S. A., *Notes and Queries*
> 6th. ser. (1880)

The Fieschi Letter

I can only suggest three theories to account for it: either it was part of a practical trick devised in the French court at the beginning of the great war to throw discredit on Edward III, and possibly to create disaffection in England; or it was the pretended confession of some person well acquainted with the circumstances of Edward's death and probably implicated in it, who wished to secure his own safety and subsistence by counterfeiting the character; or it was the real confession of a madman. There is great difficulty in the last supposition, for there is too much true and consistent detail to have been arranged by a thoroughly disordered brain; if the first be accepted, the plan of which the letter was a part must have been so completely abortive as to be otherwise unknown, and the second supposition seems almost as improbable as the authenticity of the letter.

> William Stubbs, introduction to volume 2 of the *Chronicles of Edward I and Edward II.*

The Opening of the Tomb at Gloucester

The tomb of King Edward the Second was again partially repaired in 1876. In the year 1855, some doubts having been expressed as to the actual interment of the body of the King under this tomb it was decided that an examination should be made ...:

King Edward's Tomb

On the second day of October 1855, in the presence of Dr Jeune, Canon in Residence, Mr Waller, architect, Marshall Allen, sub-sacrist, and Henry Clifford, (mason who did the work), the tomb of King Edward the Second, in the Cathedral, was opened by removing the floor on the south side of the tomb, and excavating about two feet, then working under the tomb; and only just below the flooring immediately under the tomb we came first to a wooden coffin, quite sound, and after removing a portion of this, we came to a leaden one, containing the remains of the king; the wood although light as cork, was still very perfect, and the lead one quite entire, and made with a very thick sheet of lead, its shape very peculiar, being square at bottom, and rising on each side like an arch, and so turned over the body in an oval or arched form, and seemed to have been made to set nearly close upon the body. The tomb was never known to have been opened before this. It remained open but the space of two hours, and was then closed again, without the slightest injury being done to the tomb—the fact of his interment being now 528 years since, it was considered to be in a wonderful state of preservation.

Oct. 3rd, 1855   Marshall Allen,
Cathedral, Gloucester   Sub-sacrist

Quoted from Mr Allen's notebook in H. Haines, revised F. S. Waller, *A Guide to the Cathedral Church of Gloucester*, 3rd edn. Oxford/London n. d. (1884). The original is in the Gloucester Record Office.

A Possible Solution?

WE ARE READY TO RESUME our chairs in Ashburnham drawing room under the now distinctly querulous gaze of the first Elizabeth. That queen who once recognised herself in the hapless Richard II, would have been even more discountenanced by the tortuous career and bitter fate of his great-grandfather, Edward II, as depicted in her closing years by Marlowe.

William Camden who, as head master, spent some years in the neighbourhood of this place, and whose works are in consequence housed within it, edited the 'de la More chronicle', an exemplar ready for the nineteenth century Bishop Stubbs when he came to provide his own edition for the Rolls Series. One wonders how Camden, that staid master of the *Britannia* and biographer of '*The Most Renowned and Victorious Princess Elizabeth*', now accounted by some to be the 'father of modern British historiography', would have reacted to the present complexities, seemingly more fiction than fact. Complexities, incidentally, to which his informant, Baker, masquerading as 'de la More', has contributed in excessive measure. At least the modern prober of this affair has the bulk of historical source material available in print; some of it quite unknown to Camden, in whose days much had to be laboriously recovered from the relative obscurity of manuscripts scattered throughout the land. Some of this newly available material, such as Howel ap Gruffydd's appeal, Berkeley's letter, and above all the Fieschi document, unfortunately seems to have created almost as many problems as it has solved.

An important element in the jigsaw is the differing ways in which individual pieces are viewed by the parties concerned. Mortimer, for instance, who clearly did not believe Edward of Caernarvon to be alive—otherwise he would not have acted as he did—circulated the notion that he was. The Archbishop of York took advantage of that rumour, or so we may speculate, to come to the assistance of those who had always regretted the displacement of Edward II and were now turning that regret into a positive hostility towards an unpopular regime. At a somewhat later time the same story of Edward's sojourn at Corfe, though with a happy outcome, appears in a quite different context in the Fieschi letter. The former king is now more of a cult figure in line with the Christ-like sufferer of Baker's chronicle. Perhaps we have a clue here.

It would not be fruitful to review all the conflicting evidence; most readers may already have made up their own minds as to its interpretation. But one central matter, crucial to the Fieschi letter's credibility, should be looked at. It is the supposed burial of the porter's body at Gloucester in place of the king's. We may well question whether such a substitution was possible, particularly bearing in mind the length of time that the corpse was exposed to view. Numerous people in Gloucester and the surrounding area were fully acquainted with the royal appearance, that by all accounts, and by the evidence of the effigy on his tomb—even allowing for artistic licence—was distinctive enough. Abbot Thoky tells an anecdote about Edward II's dining in the abbatial hall at St Peter's. Looking round at the paintings of his predecessors on the walls (an interesting revelation in itself) the king is said to have asked whether his portrait would be placed among them. To this the abbot responded, with a prophetic touch, that he hoped he would be in a more exalted place than that. And so it turned out. Prophecy apart, the story underlines the fact that the sight of the monarch was no uncommon thing. It follows that those local abbots and priors who were summoned to see the corpse were unlikely to be easily deceived. It could hardly be that this particular gatekeeper happened to be the king's double. Even Edward's practice of agrarian and mechanical pursuits would not have given him the appearance of a man likely to have been accustomed to hardship and to the rigours of manual labour from his earliest youth.

Moreover, if the porter were killed by Edward at his hasty departure would he not have shown signs of his violent death? There is another matter worth raising in this connection. Some have felt uneasy about the Fieschi letter's allegation that Edward made good his escape by the simple expedient of killing but one gatekeeper. Surely this is far-fetched, there must have been a number of such guards to be encountered by any would-be escapee? That there is nothing inherently impossible in the suggestion is vouched for by the fact that Robert Walkfare, a prominent Lancastrian supporter, escaped in exactly this manner, and from Corfe Castle! We know this because he was subsequently pardoned for breaking out of royal custody and for the concomitant homicide. Indeed, it could be that this particular incident was known to the compiler of the Fieschi letter. Certainly Manuele Fieschi was in a position to hear all about Walkfare's adventure.

Lastly, but not least in this connection, Isabelle if no one else must have had access to the truth. Did she not cast at least a glance at the embalmed body as it lay at Gloucester? She was certainly there. Did she not discuss its preparation with the eviscerator? Above all, if in anticipation of a holy end among the Franciscans she chose to have the heart buried with her, a sign of looked-for reunion in the hereafter and perhaps of belated repentance, did she not believe it to be her husband's? Surely she did. Yet even here we are on quicksands, for some have regarded this romantic story as no more than a pious legend, only committed to writing in the early-sixteenth century.

On a somewhat different tack, could Mortimer have hoodwinked so many eminent persons, some trained in the universities, others well acquainted with the realities of political life, so that they actually believed the extraordinary story that his *pessimi exploratores* spread abroad? Some were undoubtedly deceived, presumably Kent among them, for he confessed as much; others merely thought to take advantage of the opportunity to gather support for an insurrection, as Mortimer hoped. More circumspect men and the less gullible, such as Stratford, showed no sign of joining the ranks of the injudicious or credulous. They preferred to wait upon events. The whole business of the 'Kent conspiracy', if such a muddle of wishful thinking can be dignified by that title, becomes more believable if we regard it in terms of a frustrated opposition. It was the aftermath of the 1329 rebellion, in which most of the actors were the same, and a prelude to the *coup d'état* of October 1330, engineered by a new group of younger men attached not to the old but to the new king. This last was successful not merely because of Mortimer's removal but on account of the basic loyalty of the country to Edward III.

How then can we explain the Fieschi letter, if at all? It could not have formed any part of Mortimer's machinations, if only because his purpose was to fabricate a 'king' close at hand, rather than in the innocuous remoteness of Italy. Nonetheless there seems to be a strong possibility that the letter owes more than a little to the tales disseminated by Mortimer and luxuriantly retailed by the chroniclers. One has in addition to remember that there was an established genre, a literature of resurrected, or likely to be resurrected kings. Arthur may provide the British prototype, many others were to follow. The reappearance of Harold II, the loser at Hastings, and, in the future, of Richard II, are well attested. Examples could be multiplied for both England and the continent. In this context Edward II's return is not so remarkable after all.

The political circumstances of fourteenth-century Europe could conceivably provide some way out of our dilemma. There is no apparent connection of the Fieschi letter with France, the most obvious candidate for the rôle of fabricator. The papacy would be a more likely line of enquiry. About the time the letter was penned Edward III was in process of allying himself with the emperor Louis IV of Bavaria against Philip VI, the Valois 'occupant' of the throne of France. Edward's regnal year 1340–1341 was accounted the fourteenth of his rule over England, the first over France, the country of which he proceeded to adopt the arms and title. Pope John XXII had excommunicated the 'soi-disant emperor' and his successor, Benedict XII, pursued the same policy. Louis had responded by creating an antipope of his own. It will be noticed from the map that the story of the murder of Edward II and of the pursuit of his reputed murderer must have been well known in Genoa, which is not so far from Pisa. The ship carrying the re-captured Gurney could have passed within sight of Maguelonne. Only a short distance to the north lies Avignon. The scene is certainly right, for the future Bishop of Vercelli was at home in the whole of this area. At the same time, if we re-read the Fieschi letter it becomes manifest that we are not reading about a political saviour, a man likely to be the focus of rebellion. What we have is a holy man bent on repentance for his misdeeds, dedicated to prayer for his family, and destined to die in the odour of sanctity. Such a person could not be a political embarrassment to Edward

III, hence the letter was not an appropriate weapon for use in the papacy's diplomatic arsenal.

There is an alternative explanation, already adumbrated. We have observed that many of the political figures of Edward II's reign, such as Winchelsey (though he would have rejected the description in company with his recent biographer) and Lancaster were postulated as appropriate objects of veneration, indeed of formal canonisation. So too was Edward II. His mysterious and unedifying death led people to forget his tyranny as a ruler and the downright incompetence that had promoted disorder. As the St Albans chronicler gratefully albeit incongruously expressed it in the abbey's Book of Benefactors:

> Edward of Caernarvon, whom the Lord especially blessed in our times, and is numbered among the saints, always protected this monastery with royal power and honoured it with numerous gifts.

Edward's sumptuous tomb at Gloucester, like St Albans a Benedictine house, was to become a shrine to which flocked numerous pilgrims, Edward III among them. Here I think we approach as close to an explanation as we are likely to. The Fieschi letter is to be interpreted as a contribution to this pious cult. Instead of the horrors portrayed with extravagant precision (could we suggest zest?) by Baker, we have the serene picture of a saintly hermit living out a life of holy contemplation. All very appropriate to the myth in process of creation. This leaves Fieschi himself in a more constructive light. No longer is he subversive, rather a forwarder of a pious cult which might well have earned Edward III's respect. Always assuming he wrote the letter and that Edward received it!

The inner lead coffin thought to contain Edward II's remains (rather than the porter's) has seemingly not been opened—the Gloucester record is tantalisingly unspecific—as so many mediaeval tombs have been. That is, if we ignore the curious and unsubstantiated addition to the plaque at Sant' Alberto. The present unraveller, for one, suspects that the royal bones lie there much as they did in the earlier fourteenth century rather than in the jumbled heap to be expected had they to been transported furtively from Italy. One day this assumption may either be confirmed or disproved and that aspect of the mystery reopened or laid finally to rest.

Edward in death fared far better than in life, not only because of the many who came to his tomb and of the miracles that were wrought there, but primarily because of the rebuilding of the eastern limb of the abbey church which the steady flow of offerings made possible. Today the visitor, having first contemplated the sombre austerity of the static Norman nave, passes through the heavy stone pulpitum that serves to divide the church into two distinctive parts, and emerges with astonishment into the breathtaking glory of the luminous choir soaring above him. He will, I trust, be grateful to Edward II for this wonder of perpendicular architecture ingeniously encasing the original Norman structure. I leave it to the reader to cope with the other controversy, the place that Gloucester's choir must be given in the evolution of that architectural style, at one time considered peculiarly English and, moreover, to have risen like a phoenix for the first time in that abbey church.

Who's Who in the Story

Kings and Queens

Edward I, King 1272–1307.
Died at Burgh-on-Sands, much acclaimed but leaving a difficult legacy to his son, notably the unresolved problems of Scotland and Gascony.

Edward II, King 1307–1327.
Homosexual proclivities, considered unsuitable for kingship by a great many writers past and present. The learned author of a recent book has attempted, not in my view entirely convincingly, to explain Edward's conduct solely in terms of a compact of brotherhood (such as that between Roland and Oliver, and analogous to that of David and Jonathan). Edward's character is summarised in English by Trevisa from Ralph Higden, a later chronicler. Until 1312 much swayed by Piers Gaveston then, after an interval, by the younger Despenser. Forced in 1327 to surrender the crown to his son. Imprisoned first at Kenilworth, then at Berkeley, momentarily at Corfe Castle. Said to have escaped from Berkeley to Corfe and subsequently to have led a life as pilgrim and hermit. Supposed to have died at the abbey of Sant' Alberto di Butrio in Lombardy.

Edward III, King 1327–1377.
Son of Edward II and Isabelle of France. Crosses to France in 1325 and is kept there by his mother to his father's annoyance. Returned to England with an invasion force, mainly of Hainaulters, September 1326. Crowned king 1 February 1327. Under the tutelage of Isabelle and Mortimer 1328–1330. *Coup d'état* of October 1330 inaugurates his personal rule. Showed considerable anxiety to

capture Gurney but was lenient towards Maltravers and Berkeley. Claimed to be king of France from 1340. In 1328 he sought papal confirmation for the appropriation of three churches to Gloucester Abbey for the support of three monks to say masses for his father's soul and to celebrate the latter's anniversary.

Isabelle, daughter of Philip IV *le bel* **and sister of Charles IV, King of France (1322–1328).**
Married Edward II in 1308, probably aged twelve. Went to France in 1325 in connection with negotiations concerning Gascony and homage due for English continental possessions. Joined by Prince Edward. Liaison with Roger Mortimer developed. Returned to England with an army September 1326. Died 1358, and buried with her husband's heart in the church of the Franciscans in London, according to the tradition written down about 1526.

Popes

John XXII (Jacques Duèse), Pope 1316–1334.
The Earl of Kent visited him and the chroniclers record that he broached the subject of Edward II being still alive. John subsequently discredited the suggestion that Kent could have been believed in view of his having attended the former king's public funeral. Opponent of the Emperor Louis IV, whom he excommunicated, and critical of Edward III for assuming the vicariate of the empire and adopting the title and arms of the king of France.

Benedict XII (Jacques Fournier), Pope 1334–1342.
Followed John XXII's policy of opposing Edward III's alignment with Louis of Bavaria. Attempted mediation between Edward and Philip VI of France (reigned 1328–1350).

Bishops

Henry Burghersh, Bishop of Lincoln (1320–1340), Royal Treasurer (1327–1328), Chancellor (1328–1330).

One of the so-called *alumpni Jezebele* according to the prejudiced Baker, the other being Orleton. His relatives suffered at the hands of Edward II. Strong supporter of Isabelle and Mortimer. Said to have been in Nottingham Castle when the latter was taken prisoner in 1330. Died 1340, a trusted councillor of Edward III.

William Melton, Archbishop of York (1317–1340), Royal Treasurer (1325–1326, 1330–1331), Keeper of the Great Seal (1333–1334).

A loyal supporter of Edward II and a member of the council deputed to attend his young son. In 1328 he issued an indulgence of forty days for the late king, who had died of a 'fatal accident' (*fatalis casus*). In all churches of his diocese masses were to be sung for Edward's soul and every priest was to celebrate three such masses before Christmas. Implicated in the affair (1330) of Edmund of Woodstock, Earl of Kent, Melton subsequently claimed damages for false accusation, though one chronicler alleges that he fearlessly admitted his involvement. After his death his executor founded two chantries, one of them in York Minster where two priests were to remember the soul of Edward of Caernarvon who had helped Melton to greatness. [For his biography see W. H. Dixon and J. Raine, *Lives of the Archbishops of York*, London 1863.]

Adam Orleton, Bishop of Hereford (1317), of Worcester (1327) and of Winchester (1333–1345).

Accounted by some a friend of the Mortimers. Favourable to Isabelle, denounced by Baker as the architect of Edward of Caernarvon's fall and death. Dispute erupted with Stratford (1333) following Orleton's translation to Winchester. Can be shown not to have sent an enigmatic message to Berkeley leading to Edward's death. On the whole much maligned both in his own time and subsequently.

Walter Reynolds, Bishop of Worcester (1308), Archbishop of Canterbury (1313–1327), Royal Chancellor (1310–1314).

Usually considered a 'creature' of Edward II, whose efforts brought the rejection of the Canterbury monks' candidate, the distinguished scholar Thomas de Cobham. On the other hand, it has been argued that he constructively sought to prevent friction between the king and the church. A trimmer in 1326, but joined Isabelle when her success was assured.

Walter Stapeldon, Bishop of Exeter (1308–1326), Royal Treasurer (1320–1321, 1322–1325).

Accompanies Prince Edward to France in 1325. Despised by Isabelle as a minion of the younger Despenser and for keeping her short of money in France. Murdered by a mob while seeking sanctuary at St Paul's. Founder of Exeter College, Oxford (formerly Stapeldon Hall). His tomb is in Exeter Cathedral.

John Stratford, Bishop of Winchester (1323), Archbishop of Canterbury (1333–1348), Deputy Treasurer (1326), Royal Chancellor (1330–1334, 1335–1337, 1340).

Prominent in the deposition of Edward II. Had visited Isabelle on official business in France but did not immediately adopt her cause. Opposed Orleton's translation to Winchester (1333). Orleton in a vigorous attack emphasised Stratford's rôle in the political revolution of 1326–1327. Accounted a 'Lancastrian'.

Barons

Bartholomew Badlesmere, Steward of the Royal Household (1318–1321).

His wife, Margaret de Clare, held Leeds Castle in Kent against Queen Isabelle who had demanded entry. With a rare bout of energy Edward besieged and captured it in October 1321. He was caught and executed after the barons' defeat at Boroughbridge (1322). An uncle of Henry Burghersh, Bishop of Lincoln.

Guy De Beauchamp, Earl of Warwick.

Nicknamed 'Black dog of Arden' by the favourite Gaveston, whom the earl consequently threatened to 'bite'. Prime mover in Gaveston's abduction from the Earl of Pembroke's custody and his subsequent killing in collusion with Lancaster. Allegedly a man of culture but with an unscrupulous side.

Thomas De Berkeley, Lord Berkeley, son of Maurice de Berkeley (died 1326).

In his early manhood engaged in a large-scale riot at Painswick in Gloucestershire, property of the Earl of Pembroke. Imprisoned in the Tower and elsewhere during Edward II's reign. Married Margaret. daughter of Roger Mortimer of Wigmore, paramour of Queen Isabelle. His lands restored 1327 and in April he received custody of Edward of Caernarvon with his brother-in-law, John Maltravers. Claimed in 1330 that he knew nothing about Edward's death. A jury of knights, apparently prejudiced in his favour, found for him on all counts, but further proceedings followed. His alibi of being absent from Berkeley at the crucial time can be faulted. Undoubtedly he lied. Finally acquitted in 1337, he died in 1361.

Humphrey De Bohun, Earl of Hereford.

Favourably treated in Baker's chronicle as an honourable knight, an opinion which seems to have been general. Ally of Mortimers in the 1321–1322 rebellion. Joins Lancaster but killed ignominiously by a Welsh pikeman at Boroughbridge (1322). The Bohun family came into possession of Baker's *Chronicon*, the sole 'complete' copy.

Thomas of Brotherton, Earl of Norfolk, Earl Marshal.

Said by Fieschi to have been lord of Chepstow Castle. Although he was Edward II's half-brother he quickly joined Isabelle in 1326. Involved in the abortive rebellion of 1329. Died in 1338.

Gilbert De Clare, Earl of Gloucester.

Died fighting bravely but rashly at Bannockburn (1314), leaving three sisters as coheiresses. The eldest, Eleanor, wife of the younger Hugh Despenser, who apparently had an affair with King Edward, married secondly La Zouche Mortimer who besieged Caerphilly Castle in 1326–1327.

Hugh Le Despenser, the elder, created Earl of Winchester 1322.

Had served Edward I and was far less in evidence than his son, but nonetheless widely hated by the end of Edward II's reign. Defended Bristol against Isabelle in 1326, but forced to surrender and was put to death.

Hugh Le Despenser, the younger.

Married Eleanor de Clare, eldest of the Gloucester co-heiresses. Attempted to acquire Gower and had ambitions to be Earl of Gloucester. Hence he antagonised his brothers-in-law Hugh Audley and Roger Damory. Favourite of Edward II and according to the Lanercost chronicle 'as though his right eye' (*quasi oculus dexter*). Was virtual controller of the government after Borough-bridge (1322). Became widely hated for his exactions. Put to death in gruesome circumstances at Hereford in 1326. These, as related in detail by Froissart, following Jean le Bel, can be matched by twelfth-century examples from York and may reflect the nature of his 'crimes'.

Piers Gaveston, created Earl of Cornwall 1307.

Companion of Edward of Caernarvon's youth and early manhood. A Gascon and considered to be 'alien', although Gascony was an important part of the English king's dominions. Created an unfavourable sensation at Edward II's coronation by his extravagant and bizarre attire. Kept prisoner by the Earl of Pembroke under safe conduct but he was abducted from Deddington rectory in Oxfordshire and killed (1312) at the instigation of the Earls of Warwick and Lancaster. Buried at the royal foundation of Kings Langley after the body had remained for some time with their fellow Dominicans at Oxford.

Henry of Lancaster, Earl of Leicester and Lancaster.

Younger brother of Thomas whom he succeeded. Said to have been a considerate custodian of his kinsman Edward at his castle of Kenilworth. After Edward III's coronation (1327) drifted into a quarrel with Mortimer during a struggle for power. This led to an armed confrontation at Winchester (1328) and to the unsuccessful rebellion of 1329. Lost his sight, died in 1345.

Thomas of Lancaster, Earl of Leicester and Lancaster and of three other earldoms.

Elder brother of Henry. A rather sullen character. Led baronial opposition to Edward II somewhat fitfully. Tried to enforce Ordinances on the king. Failed to relieve Leeds Castle (1321). Besieged the royal castle of Tickhill, but defeated at Boroughbridge (1322) and put to death ignominiously. Movement for his canonisation developed following reports of miracles at Pontefract. The Earl of Kent advocated this at Avignon.

John Maltravers, a Dorset baron from Lytchett, Steward of the Royal Household (1328, 1329–1330).

Held lands in Oxfordshire, Berkshire, Somersetshire and Wiltshire as well as in Dorset. With the Berkeleys in a riot at Painswick (1319), the Earl of Pembroke's property, and with Mortimer for the burning of Bridgnorth during the 1321–1322 rebellion. Acted against the Despensers in the Welsh March; escaped abroad after Boroughbridge. His lands restored in 1327. Associated with his brother-in-law Berkeley in the custody of Edward II at Berkeley Castle. Popular opinion held him guilty of the murder. However, the 1330 parliament did not convict him of that crime, but only of encompassing the death of the Earl of Kent. A price of £500 was put on his head. Agent of Mortimer in suggesting that Edward remained alive. Escaped abroad and served Edward III in Flanders. Given safe conduct to England in 1345; this renewed in 1347. His outlawry revoked in 1351 owing to his services abroad. He died in 1364.

Roger Mortimer of Wigmore, created first Earl of the March in 1328.

Involved in the 1321–1322 rebellion. Given a safe conduct but taken and imprisoned in the Tower, from which he escaped in 1323 by drugging his guards. Despite suggestions adopted by

Marlowe among others, there is no evidence of a liaison with Queen Isabelle prior to her arrival in France (1325). Stayed behind the scenes for Edward II's deposition. Real ruler of the country with Isabelle 1328–1330. Captured by William de Montacute (Montagu), later Earl of Salisbury, in Nottingham Castle (October) and condemned in the November 1330 parliament. Among his alleged crimes were those of effecting Edward II's death and deceiving the Earl of Kent to provide excuse for his death. The remains of his castle of Wigmore have recently been 'consolidated' by English Heritage. His uncle, also Roger, who died in the Tower, was from nearby Chirk, where the outer walls of the castle are still impressive.

Edmund of Woodstock, Earl of Kent.

Half-brother of Edward II. A weak character. Involved in 1329 rebellion against Isabelle and Mortimer and later led to believe that Edward of Caernarvon was alive. Wrote an incriminating letter soon used against him. Condemned at the Winchester parliament and executed (1330).

Chroniclers

Geoffrey Le Baker, clerk, of Swinbrook, Oxfordshire.

Wrote the *Chronicon* and a brief *Chroniculum* or little chronicle—scarcely more than a series of factual statements. That part of his major chronicle covering Edward II's reign was for long attributed to a knight, 'de la More'. [See Sir Thomas de la More below] Baker gives graphic accounts of the abuse of Edward of Caernarvon and of his death at Berkeley. He is not reliable for Edward II's reign or for details of Gurney's flight. A propagandist?

Walter Frocester, Abbot of St Peter's, Gloucester.

This abbot, who died in 1412—we have his funeral oration—is thought to have been responsible for a *Historia* of his house (Rolls Series). This includes material about Edward II, an anecdote recalling his visit in Abbot Thoky's time and the latter's arrangements for the transfer of the corpse from Berkeley.

Jean Le Bel, Canon of Liège.

He was an eyewitness of some of the events of 1326–1327. His chronicle is therefore invaluable for the period and was much used by Froissart. Only available in French: *Chronique de Jean le Bel*, ed. J. Viard and E. Déprez, 2 vols. Paris 1904–5.

Jean Froissart, clerk.

'French' chronicler born in Valenciennes (Hainault) in the 1330s, died in the decade after 1400. A great admirer of Edward III, the earlier part of his chronicle is based on that of Jean le Bel. He stayed in England during the 1360s and for a short time during Richard II's reign. On the earlier occasion he visited Berkeley and expressed curiosity about the fate of Edward II. There is a modern translation by Brereton. The most manageable edition in French is *Froissart, Jean, Chroniques*, ed. S. Luce, G. Reynaud, Paris 1869–99.

Sir Thomas (Laurence) De La More, of Northmoor, Oxfordshire.

He is called 'nephew' of Bishop Stratford in whose retinue he travelled to Kenilworth. In fact it is only the account of this particular incident which is attributable to him. The so-called 'de la More chronicle' is in fact a version of Baker's.

Adam Murimuth, Canon of St Paul's.

He probably came from Fifield in Oxfordshire, hence he would have been Baker's neighbour and More's. Baker uses his chronicle as a base until 1341. Somewhat envious of his more successful colleagues, such as Orleton. His work is on the whole careful and judicious, being related to the so-called Pauline annals, a somewhat motley compilation. He declared that Edward's body was displayed but implied that it was not clearly seen.

Men convicted of Edward of Caernarvon's murder

Sir Thomas Gurney or Gournay

of Inglis(h)combe (now Englishcombe) in Somerset—where the family has given its name to the villages Barrow Gurney and Farrington Gurney. He also held property in Oxfordshire and elsewhere. A descendant of Robert de Gurney co-founder of St Mark's Hospital, Bristol, now the Lord Mayor's Chapel.

Engaged in riotous behaviour with the Berkeleys and Maltravers (1319–1320). Pardoned in 1324, but made to undertake substantial recognisances in favour of the elder Despenser. These were cancelled in 1328 as having been imposed by duress. In 1331 his wife Joan received support from forfeited dower lands in Wiltshire and Somerset and subsequently was permitted to rent most of her husband's confiscated estates. He fled abroad in 1331 by way of Cornwall. Imprisoned at Burgos, he escaped. Recaptured at Naples. He died in Bayonne. His embalmed body was taken back to Tynemouth (1333), presumably for inspection by Edward III, then campaigning in the north. His famous son, Sir Matthew de Gurney, who died in 1406, when he was said to be 96, was a notable warrior during the Hundred Years War and is mentioned admiringly by Froissart.

Roger Mortimer of Wigmore. See under Barons

William Ockley, from Ireland.

Surprisingly little can be discovered about this man. Lands in Ireland were restored to him in 1327, an indication that he had been a rebel against Edward II. In 1326 he was attorney in Ireland for Stephen de Ockley, presumably a relative. A man of this name was custodian of Joan, wife of Roger Mortimer, in 1322. If he was this Ockley he must have become a rebel subsequently. Allegedly sent by Mortimer from Abergavenny to Berkeley with Shalford's letter, which supposedly determined the murder. Made keeper of Ellesmere manor, Shropshire, by Queen Isabelle. Laurence of

Ludlow, knight, pardoned in 1332 for stealing his goods, he (Ockley) being a rebel. Ultimate fate unknown. His relationship to the Ogle family of the north-east of England is unclear, but has sometimes been assumed or implied.

Mortimer's henchmen

Sir Simon Bereford or Barford, of Leicestershire.

In rebellion against Edward II. Some history of violence, presumably on that account. His property confiscated 1324. Pardoned in 1327 for trespasses, homicides and other offences. Granted manor of Latimer (*Iselhampstede*) for service to Isabelle as well as the Despenser manor of Fritheby, Leicestershire. Acted as escheator from 1328. Associated with Kent's deception. Bailiff of Tickhill, a royal castle in Yorkshire. Condemned in 1330 as one associated in Mortimer's crimes and put to death. Had left £2000 with the prior of Tackley at his house in Cripplegate, London, in case he managed to escape.

Sir John Deveril, of Dorset.

His father was Elias Deveril. He married Elizabeth, but later (1313–1314) was 'divorced' owing to consanguinity. Involved in the looting of Bindon Abbey in Dorset by a mob (1329). Concerned as constable of Corfe with Kent's deception. He was condemned in the 1330 parliament. In 1331 was thought to be hiding in the Dorset-Somerset area. The same price, 100 marks alive or £40 dead, was put on his head as on that of Ockley.

John Maltravers of Lytchett. See under Barons

William Shalford, deputy-justice of North Wales under Mortimer.

Accused by Howel ap Gruffydd of sending a letter in September 1327 warning Mortimer, then at Abergavenny, of threatened Welsh risings in conjunction with others in England. Judgment was eventually given for the defendant, who continued in Edward III's confidence. Possibly this was merely an attempt by 'loyalist Welsh' to discredit him.

Sir John Wysham, Steward of the Household (1328–1329), Justice of North Wales (1330–1331).

Appeal against Shalford brought before him. Eventually heard in King's Bench and Chancery courts. Supporter of Mortimer, but made royal keeper of his forfeited lands by Edward III. He was also in favour with William de Montacute.

Welshmen

Howel Ap Gruffydd.

In 1331 he brought an appeal against William de Shalford, which alleged he had sent a letter to Mortimer which precipitated Edward of Caernarvon's death. An associate of Gruffydd Llwyd, a staunch supporter of Edward II. Both arrested at Caernarvon in 1327.

Llywelyn Ap Gruffydd *alias* Llywelyn Bren.

It has been suggested that he could have been a son of Gruffydd ap Rhys of Senghenydd. In 1316 he attacked Caerphilly and captured the sheriff of Glamorgan, its constable. Two years later he was tried in Despenser's court and suffered a traitor's death at Cardiff. As a result his sons and his wife supported Mortimer and others in devastating the Despenser lordship in the area (1321).

Sir Rhys Ap Gruffydd, from West Wales.

He was often employed as an arrayer of troops for Edward II and was with him at Neath in 1326, when he was used as an envoy to Henry of Lancaster. He subsequently received a pardon. Mentioned in Howel ap Gruffydd's appeal as leading a revolt (1327) in South Wales. Amongst other things accused of being an adherent of the Scots.

William Le Galeys.

Name used by a man at Cologne who professed to be Edward II. Taken to Edward III at Coblence and then seemingly to Antwerp. No further record of him.

Various

Bogo (Boeges) of Bayeux (*de Boicis*) or of Bayonne (*De Baion'*).
Probably he should be included among Mortimer's henchmen.
Apparently a northern knight and rebel against Edward II, since
his lands were restored in 1327 by the sheriffs of Yorkshire and
Northumberland. Condemned with Maltravers and on the same
charge, causing the death of Kent.

William Beaukaire, Royal Sergeant-at-arms.
He arrived at Berkeley Castle on the day of Edward's death. Paid
to stay with the body while it lay at Gloucester. Possibly the man
(though his first name is uncertain) who was in the garrison at
Caerphilly. It is probably pure coincidence that Beaucaire is a place
near Maguelonne!

Stephen Dunheved, the brother of Friar Thomas.
At one time held Dunchurch manor near Rugby and property in
Dunsmore near Kenilworth. Involved with his brother in attempts
to rescue Edward II. Both are mentioned in Berkeley's letter of
1327. Imprisoned at Newgate, London, but escaped. Rearrested in
1329.

Br Robert De Beby, Benedictine monk.
Sent from Westminster Abbey in 1327 to try to secure the body
of Edward II for burial there. His expense roll is among the abbey
muniments.

William Bishop, Royal Sergeant in charge of Edward's escort to Berkeley.
Baker alleges that this man was responsible for the degrading
cruelties inflicted on the former king and that he told the chronicler
about it after the Black Death, having performed penance and in
the hope of God's mercy. A man of this all too common name
was pardoned for acting against the Despensers (1321) and was
rioting at Warwick (1323). A sergeant-at-arms of the same name

in Edward III's service is recorded in the patent rolls from 1338 until after the Black Death.

Br Richard Bliton, Carmelite friar.

Despenser's confessor. On the boat with him in the Bristol Channel and implicated in the 'Kent conspiracy'.

Master Pancius De Controne, Italian physician.

He was royal physician to Edward II, Isabelle and later Edward III and well rewarded for his services. Significantly he did not attend the former king in prison.

William De Cornwell (Cornwall?), an esquire.

Attaches Gurney by suit in the court of the king of Sicily at Naples. Armour was brought to him by Thweng. Whether or not he acted on his own initiative is unclear. For his services he was made bailiff/gatekeeper of Norwich Castle.

Br Thomas Dunheved, Dominican friar, brother of Stephen.

Reputedly sent to secure from the pope a divorce between Isabelle and Edward II. Mentioned in chamber account book in the library of the Society of Antiquaries (MS 122) as carrying letters of Edward II, then in Wales, to the younger Despenser, so he was probably with the king until his capture. Imprisoned at Pontefract, but quite when is unclear. Probably dead by 1329 although the Lanercost chronicler thought he was raising the devil to ascertain whether Edward was alive. The name 'Dunheved' or 'Donheved' is found in Wiltshire and Cornwall. Downhead (*Donheved*) manor in Somerset was once held by Gurney.

Sir John Felton.

Constable of Caerphilly Castle in 1326, which he only surrendered on terms in March 1327, thus preserving the life of the junior Despenser's young son.

Manuele De Fieschi, Papal Notary, Provost of Arnhem, Canon of Salisbury etc., Bishop of Vercelli (1343).

Some biographical details are in *Hemingby's Register* (Wiltshire Record Society). Believed to be the author of a letter to Edward III of which only a copy survives. It purports to contain details of a confession made by Edward of Caernarvon, but that could be just an ingenious way of confirming the surprising information it contains. The form of the letter begs a number of questions. There is no initial address such as one would expect in a letter directed to the king, nor is it a properly attested notarial document to emphasise authenticity. Maybe that would have been too formal. There are no suitably laudable epithets in the body of the text. The style is turgid with an undue repetition of 'aforesaid', the orthography is local, said by one antiquary to be typically Genoese. But though the location may be apt, it remains open to question whether such a document could have come from the pen of a man skilled in the art of formal composition. His name could have been used by someone else.

Hugh Glanvill(e), Royal Clerk.

Responsible for making arrangements and necessary payments for Edward's lying in state. Suspicious circumstances of the omission of his journey to Worcester with the eviscerator to see Queen Isabelle.

Robert Lynel.

One of those attached by Giles of Spain in the Iberian peninsula. No information has yet been found to indicate the precise nature of the offence.

John Prikehare, clerk of Winchester diocese.

Used as a catspaw by the government in an attempt to prevent Bishop Orleton's translation to Winchester (1333). His appeal to the papal curia sought to condemn Orleton as author of many of the discredited aspects of the political revolution of 1326–1327. The pope did not take the matter seriously.

Giles of Spain, Sergeant-at-arms.

Sent to Spain and Aragon for the apprehension of Gurney 1331–1332. Although he almost succeeded, Gurney managed to escape to Italy from Burgos. Back in England Giles made a number of arrests, allegedly of men concerned with Edward II's death.

Sir William De Thweng, a Yorkshire knight.

After Giles of Spain's failure he was sent to Naples to bring back Gurney, already detained. His mission was accomplished when he made his report to the king on 7 July 1333, but Gurney had died before he set out on the return journey, so he brought back the body.

John Tilly, Squire of Sir Thomas Gurney (q.v.).

Possibly considered guilty by association. However, we know nothing of any offence with which he was charged.

John Walwayn, senior and junior.

There were two clerks of this name who have often been confused. The elder, who had died by July 1326, may have been the author of the *Vita Edwardi Secundi,* as its latest editor suggests. The case for his authorship is circumstantial but quite compelling. The younger Walwayn was previously thought to have been the author of the letter which informed Chancellor Hothum of Edward of Caernarvon's removal from Berkeley by men who also pillaged the castle. This confusion, and at least one other, has been cleared up by W. J. Smyth in his article 'The Rise of the Berkeleys', following Noel Denholm-Young.

Aids

Sketch Maps and Genealogical Tables

i. The Pursuit and Capture of Sir Thomas Gurney

ii. The supposed Journeyings of Edward of Caernarvon (Caernarfon)

England: The Descendants of King Henry III

France: The Descendants of King Philip III

Somerset: The family of Gurney

The Pursuit and Capture of Sir Thomas Gurney

KEY

Sir Thomas Gurney's escape route from Berkeley   ... ─ >... ─ >

Route taken by Sir William Thweng and the captive Gurney.   ....>........>

(1) Gurney imprisoned at Burgos.

(2) Arrest of Gurney at Naples.

(3) Gurney dies at Bayonne after illness unsuccessfully treated by his captors.

(4) His body embalmed prior to shipment from Bordeaux to Sandwich.

(5) Thweng makes landfall at Tynemouth and reports to Edward III at Berwick.

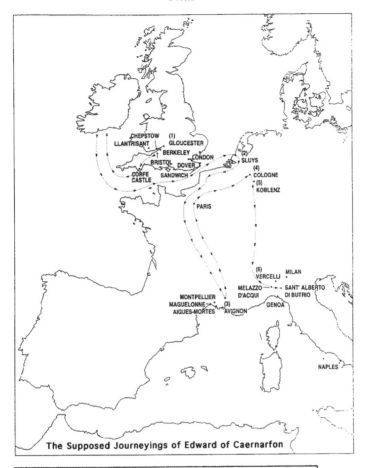

The Supposed Journeyings of Edward of Caernarfon

KEY

Edward of Caernarfon's supposed route ....>........>........>........>

(1) Burial of the body of King Edward II at St. Peter's Abbey, Gloucester

(2) The route adopted assumes that Edward of Caernarfon would have travelled from Ireland to Sandwich by sea rather than landing on the west coast and following the more dangerous overland route. The Fieschi letter merely states that he returned (redivit) to England and touched (applicuit) at Sandwich before crossing to Sluys.

(3) Edward meets Pope John XXII at Avignon.

(4) Edward makes a pilgrimage to the shrine of the Three Kings at Cologne. Interestingly the sole dedication to the Magi in England appears to have been the chapel, founded in 1504 and still surviving, attached to John Foster's hospital in Bristol.

(5) Edward III made vicar of the Empire by Louis IV in September 1338

(6) Manuele de Fieschi promoted bishop of Vercelli in 1343.

England

Henry III = Eleanor of Provence
(1216–1272)

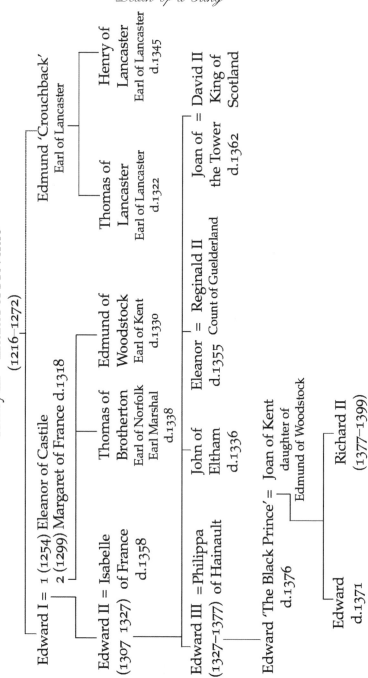

France

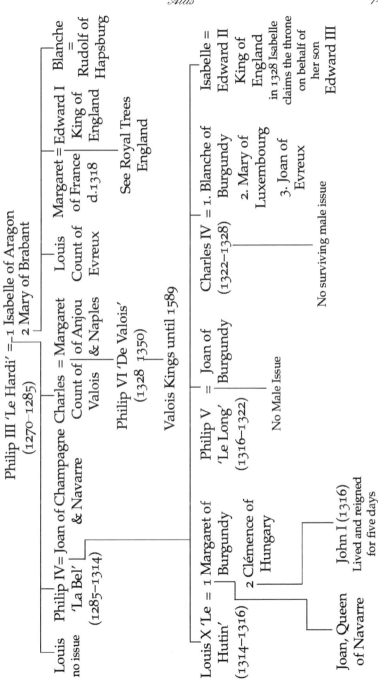

Philip III 'Le Hardi' =⎡1 Isabelle of Aragon
(1270–1285) ⎣2 Mary of Brabant

Louis
no issue

Philip IV = Joan of Champagne
'La Bel' & Navarre
(1285–1314)

Charles = Margaret
Count of of Anjou
Valois & Naples

Louis
Count of
Evreux

Margaret = Edward I
of France King of
d.1318 England

Blanche
=
Rudolf of
Hapsburg

See Royal Trees
England

Isabelle = Edward II
King of
England
in 1328 Isabelle
claims the throne
on behalf of
her son
Edward III

Philip VI 'De Valois'
(1328–1350)

Valois Kings until 1589

Charles IV = 1. Blanche of
(1322–1328) Burgundy
2. Mary of
Luxembourg
3. Joan of
Evreux

No surviving male issue

Louis X 'Le = ⎡1 Margaret of
Hutin' ⎢ Burgundy
(1314–1316) ⎣2 Clémence of
Hungary

Philip V = Joan of
'Le Long' Burgundy
(1316–1322)

No Male Issue

John I (1316)
Lived and reigned
for five days

Joan, Queen
of Navarre

A branch of the Gurney (Gournay) family of Somerset

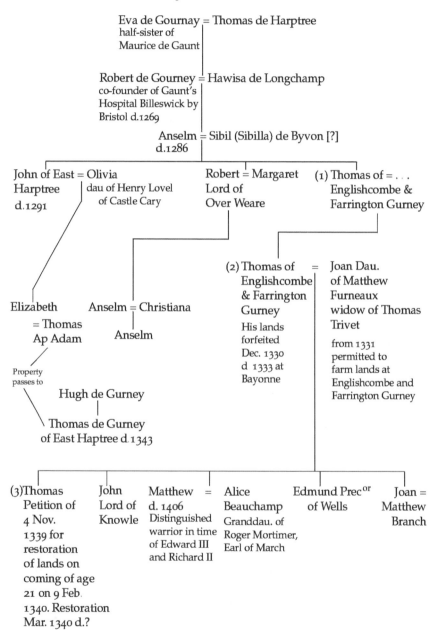

Eva de Gournay = Thomas de Harptree
half-sister of
Maurice de Gaunt

Robert de Gourney = Hawisa de Longchamp
co-founder of Gaunt's
Hospital Billeswick by
Bristol d.1269

Anselm = Sibil (Sibilla) de Byvon [?]
d.1286

John of East = Olivia
Harptree   dau of Henry Lovel
d.1291   of Castle Cary

Robert = Margaret
Lord of
Over Weare

(1) Thomas of = . . .
Englishcombe &
Farrington Gurney

(2) Thomas of   =   Joan Dau.
Englishcombe   of Matthew
& Farrington   Furneaux
Gurney   widow of Thomas
His lands   Trivet
forfeited
Dec. 1330   from 1331
d 1333 at   permitted to
Bayonne   farm lands at
                     Englishcombe and
                     Farrington Gurney

Elizabeth   Anselm = Christiana
= Thomas
Ap Adam   Anselm

Property
passes to
        Hugh de Gurney

        Thomas de Gurney
        of East Haptree d.1343

(3)Thomas   John   Matthew =   Alice   Edmund Prec^or   Joan =
Petition of   Lord of   d. 1406   Beauchamp   of Wells   Matthew
4 Nov.   Knowle   Distinguished Granddau. of   Branch
1339 for   warrior in time Roger Mortimer,
restoration   of Edward III Earl of March
of lands on   and Richard II
coming of age
21 on 9 Feb.
1340. Restoration
Mar. 1340 d.?

Sources and Suggestions for Further Reading

The fundamental starting point is the article by T. F. Tout, 'The Captivity and Death of Edward of Carnarvon', *Bulletin of the John Rylands Library* 6 (1921–1922), reprinted in *Collected Papers* 3, Manchester 1934. More recently G. P. Cuttino and T. W. Lyman have contributed the very useful 'Where is Edward II?', *Speculum* 53 (1978). This contains photographs of Sant' Alberto di Butrio and of the historiated capitals of the cloister there. It implies a degree of acceptance of the Fieschi letter, of which the Latin text is given together with a translation. Some of the bibliography in the footnotes there, being readily accessible, will not be repeated here. The latter part of the article (by Lyman) is concerned with architectural matters. Included, too, is a 'Time Table' of events in the story and a genealogical table of the Fieschi family to illustrate Manuele's relationships and the connection with the English royal family. I would certainly like to acknowledge my obligation to this article, a copy of which was sent to me by the late Professor Cuttino. However, my research over a number of years has been independent. My conclusions are quite different in a number of respects. Most of them are in my article '*Edwardus Redivivus*: the 'Afterlife' of Edward of Caernarvon, *Transactions of the Bristol & Gloucestershire Archaeological Society* [hereafter *TB&GAS*] 114 (1996), pp. 65–86.

The basic source for Gurney's pursuit, on which I have relied heavily and at a number of points entirely, is Joseph Hunter's meticulous paper in *Archaeologia* 27 (1838). This contains invaluable transcripts of the documents in the case abstracted from the public records. In volume 50 (1887) of *Archaeologia* is an article by S. A. Moore, 'Documents relating to the Death and Burial of King

Edward II'. This should be used in conjunction with John Smyth, ed. Sir John Maclean, *The Lives of the Berkeleys*, Gloucester 1883–1886 (volume 1) and Isaac H. Jeayes, *Descriptive Catalogue of the Charters and Muniments in the Possession of Lord Fitzhardinge at Berkeley Castle*, Bristol 1892, and more recently, W. J. Smith, 'The Rise of the Berkeleys: an Account of the Berkeleys of Berkeley Castle 1243–1361', *TB&GAS* 70 (1951), especially pp. 76–8, correcting Tanquerey, for whose article see below. For Gurney in Spain see volume 3 of *Acta Aragonensia*, ed. H. Finke, Berlin-Leipzig 1908–1966. Details of this family are in D. Gurney, *The Record of the House of Gournay* (London, 1848, 1858). The Somerset branch is dealt with in Part 4. An invaluable source, but too ready to accept unsupported statements of biased chroniclers.

The contributions of J. Theodore Bent and J. H. Cooke to the discussion of the Fieschi letter are in *Notes and Queries* 6th ser. 2 (1880). See also H. D. Rawnsley, 'Did Edward II escape to Italy?', *The British Review* 12 (1915). For the views of Stubbs see his introduction to volume 2 of the *Chronicles of the Reigns of Edward I and Edward II* (Rolls Series 1883).

For the Italian viewpoint see A. Benedetti, *Edoardo II d'Inghilterra all'Abbazia di S. Alberto di Butrio*, Palermo 1924, and Constantino Nigra, 'Uno degli Edoardi in Italia: Favola o Storia?', *Nuova Antologia, revista di lettere, scienze ed arti*, ser. 4, 92 (1901). Both of these references I owe to Professor Cuttino. Most of the chroniclers, including Murimuth and 'de la More' are in the Rolls Series and enumerated in 'List 24' *English National Archives* 1983, published by H. M. S. O. and obtainable free from its branches. Those that are published elsewhere include the *Brut*, edited F. W. D. Brie, *Early English Text Society*, original ser. 131, 136 (1906, 1908); the *Chronicon* of Geoffrey le Baker, is edited by E. Maunde Thompson with excellent notes, Oxford 1889. See also the *Chronicon de Lanercost*, ed. J. Stevenson, Edinburgh 1839; the *Vita Edwardi Secundi* (Latin-English text), ed. N. Denholm-Young, London 1957; Froissart's *Chronicles*, ed. Geoffrey Brereton, Harmondsworth 1968. John Stow, *The Survey of London*, is conveniently edited by H. B. Wheatley, London (Everyman) 1965, but there is no good modern version either of Holinshed's *Chronicle* or of Stow's *Annals*.

Many documents about this affair are in Thomas Rymer, *Foedera*, which appears in various editions. Calendars of the patent and close rolls, adequately indexed, are invaluable for tracing people and events. These are also in 'List 24'.

The legal proceedings arising from Howel ap Gruffydd's appeal are in an appendix to Tout's article 'The Captivity' noted above. See also F. J. Tanquerey, 'The Conspiracy of Thomas Dunheved, 1327', *English Historical Review* 21 (1916).

There are various literary allusions to Edward II apart from Marlowe and Bertolt Brecht. For Edward's lament see Paul Studer, *The Modern Language Review* 16 (1921), and T. M. Smallwood, *Modern Languages Association* 68 (1973). Adam Davy's 'Five Dreams about Edward II' are edited by E. J. Furnivall, *Early English Text Society* 1878. A number of pieces collected by Thomas Wright, *Political Songs of England*, Camden Society 1839, have reference to Edward II and his reign. For the historical background to Trevisa, the vicar of Berkeley and the Berkeleys' chaplain, who rendered Higden's *Polychronicon* into English, see D. C. Fowler, 'New Light on John Trevisa', *Traditio* 17 (1962), and more recently the same writer's *The Life and Times of John Trevisa, Medieval Scholar*, Seattle/London 1995.

Other aspects of Edward II are treated by Edward Peters, 'The Shadow King, *Rex Inutilis*' in *Medieval Law and Literature*, Yale 1970; and by Chalfont Robinson, 'Was King Edward the Second a Degenerate?', *American Journal of Insanity* 66 (1909–1910). Robinson thought that he certainly was.

For death and burial practices see C. A. Bradford, *Heart Burial*, London 1933; E. A. R. Brown, 'Death and the Human Body in the Later Middle Ages: the Legislation of Boniface VIII on the Division of the Corpse', *Viator* 12 (1981); E. M. Hallam, 'Royal Burial and the Cult of Kingship in France and England 1060–1330', *Journal of Medieval History* 8 (1982). For Isabelle's burial: C. L. Kingsford, *The Grey Friars of London: Their History with the Register of their Convent and an Appendix of Documents*, British Society of Franciscan Studies 6, Aberdeen 1915; F. D. Blackley, 'The Tomb of Isabella of France, wife of Edward II of England', *Bulletin of the International Society for the Study of Church Monuments* 8 (1983), pp. 161–4 (typescript)

For Ashburnham House, now part of Westminster School: A. L. N. Russell, *Westminster School: the Story of Ashburnham House*,

3rd edn. 1949 n. p. For Caerphilly: W. Rees, *Caerphilly Castle*, Cardiff 1937 (also enlarged 1971, 1974); C. N. Johns, *Caerphilly Castle*, H. M. S. O. Cardiff 1978 (with bibliography). For Caernarvon and Edward II: A. J. Taylor, 'The Castle of St Georges d'Espéranche', *Antiquaries Journal* 33 (1953); idem, 'The Birth of Edward of Caernarvon and the beginning of Caernarvon Castle', *History* new series 35 (1950); idem, *Caernarvon Castle and Town Walls*, H. M. S. O. London 1975. Dr Taylor's studies are now collected in *Studies in Castles and Castle-Building*, 1984. More generally, M. Prestwich, 'English Castles in the Reign of Edward II', *Journal of Medieval History* 8 (1982).

On particular points see P. C. Doherty, 'The Date of the Birth of Isabella, Queen of England', *Bulletin of the Institute of Historical Research* 48 (1975); V. H. Galbraith, 'Extracts from the *Historia Aurea* and a French *Brut*', *English Historical Review* 43 (1928)); J. Griffith, *Edward II in Glamorgan*, London 1904.

There is still no really good biography of Edward II incorporating recent research, although Seymour Phillips is preparing one for Yale University Press. T. F. Tout, revised Hilda Johnstone, *The Place of Edward II in English History*, Manchester 1936, is scholarly but selective. H. F. Hutchison, *Edward II the Pliant King*, London 1971, is a readable popular biography, while C. Bingham, *The Life and Times of Edward II*, London 1973, though not original scholarship is well illustrated. The last two have been closely followed by G. Thurlow, *Gloucester and Berkeley and the Story of Edward II Martyr King*, Norwich 1977, a booklet on sale in the cathedral.

Isabelle has been badly served by historians. A more favourable impression is given by S. Menache, 'Isabelle of France, Queen of England: a Reconsideration', *Journal of Medieval History* 10 (1984).

For Gaveston: J. S. Hamilton, *Piers Gaveston, Earl of Cornwall 1307–1312*, Detroit 1988. P. Chaplais, *Piers Gaveston, Edward II's Adoptive Brother*, Oxford 1994, argues against the view of some contemporaries and most modern historians that Edward was a homosexual.

Among books with extensive bibliographies on the period are R. M. Haines, *The Church and Politics in Fourteenth-Century England: the Career of Adam Orleton*, Cambridge 1978; idem, *Archbishop John Stratford*, Pontifical Institute of Mediaeval Studies, Toronto 1986;

N. M. Fryde, *The Tyranny and Fall of Edward II, 1321–1326*, Cambridge 1979; J. R. Wright, *The Church and the English Crown 1305–1334*, PIMS Toronto 1980. Revised biographies of many of the characters in the story will appear in the *New Dictionary of National Biography*, scheduled to appear in 2004 or shortly thereafter.